JESUS – The Prophet Who Didn't Die

An Islamic and Quranic explanation on Mary, Jesus, his Disciples, Crucifixion, and other fundamentals of Christianity

IqraSense

Other Books by IqraSense

1. Jerusalem is Ours - The centuries old Christian, Islamic, and Jewish struggle for the "Holy Lands"
2. The Power of Dua (Prayers)
3. 100+ Dua (Prayers) for Success and Happiness
4. Summarized Stories of the Quran

JESUS – The Prophet Who Didn't Die

An Islamic and Quranic explanation on Jesus, Mary, and other fundamentals of Christianity

Library of Congress Number: 2012908203

Printed in the United States of America

| ISBN: | 1477406689 |
| ISBN-13: | 978-1477406687 |

TABLE OF CONTENTS

1 Introduction 1

2 The Birth of Jesus 4

   2.1 Maryam's birth and her guardianship... 4

   2.2 Life of Maryam 7

   2.3 Birth of Jesus 8

   2.4 Maryam comes back to Jerusalem... 11

   2.5 Jesus speaks from the cradle 12

   2.6 Jews keep Jesus' miracle of speech in cradle a secret 12

3 The Life of Jesus and his Teachings 14

   3.1 Jesus' teachings.. 14

   3.2 Similarity between Jesus' real teachings and Islamic practices . 14

      3.2.1 Circumcision 16

      3.2.2 Prohibition of eating pork 18

      3.2.3 Proper animals slaughter methods 19

      3.2.4 Prohibition of Alcohol 20

      3.2.5 Ablution before prayer.. 22

      3.2.6 Prostration in prayer 23

      3.2.7 Commandments for Veiling and Covering 24

      3.2.8 Fasting.. 26

      3.2.9 Prohibition of Interest.. 27

3.2.10   Disparaging of pagan practices 27

3.3   Stories from Jesus' life 28

3.4   Jesus was an ethnic Prophet.............................31

4   Miracles of Jesus 33

4.1   Jesus speaking in the cradle as an infant 33

4.2   Allah sent a table of food for his disciples on his request.........34

4.3   Jesus could breathe life into objects made of clay 37

4.4   Healing the Blind and the Leper..........................37

4.5   Power to know what people had eaten and stored in their homes 39

5   Islamic explanation refuting Jesus as being son of God..........40

5.1   Misinterpretations about 'son of God' 42

5.2   Quran's rejection of the notion of God's son...........47

6   Islamic views on the disciples of Jesus.................49

7   Death of Jesus 53

8   The second coming of Jesus 62

9   CONCLUSION 65

10   Appendix A – Quranic verses and Chapter on Mary (Maryam) and Jesus (Isa)..66

10.1   Chapter of Baqara Quran Verses (Chapter 2) 66

10.2   Chapter Aal-Imraan Quran Verses (Chapter 3) 68

10.3   Chapter of Al-Nisaa Quran Verses (Chapter 4) 70

10.4   Chapter Al-Maaidah Quran Verses (Chapter 5) 71

10.5   Chapter Al-Aaraf Quran Verses (Chapter 7)................................74

10.6   Chapter Al-Nahl Quran Verses (Chapter 16) 74

10.7   Chapter Ash-Shuara Quran Verses (Chapter 26)........................74

10.8   Chapter Ash-Shura Quran Verses (Chapter 42) 75

10.9   Chapter As-Saff Quran Verses (Chapter 61)...............................75

10.10   Chapter of Maryam (Mary) – Complete (Chapter 19)............76

11   REFERENCES 88

About Quran and Hadith

Quran – Quran is the word of God (Allah) that was revealed to Prophet Muhammad. In Islam, Quran is a continuation of God's message for mankind that was revealed in Jewish and Christian texts. However, according to Islamic beliefs, as those texts and teachings were corrupted by people over time, Quran as the word of God (Allah) was revealed to refresh Allah's message for mankind. In Islam, therefore, while Muslims are supposed to recognize Torah and Bible as Jewish and Christian texts that were revealed by Allah, Muslims are not supposed to follow those teachings as the word of God was changed. Instead, Quran is the ultimate authoritative religious text for Muslims.

Hadith are narrations and traditions of Prophet Muhammad that Muslims are supposed to abide by as part of their daily lives. In many cases, these narrations are also a further explanation of the message of the Quran. The six major Hadith collections include the following: Sahih al-Bukhari, Sahih Muslim, Sunan Abu Dawood, Al-Sunan an-Nasai, Sunan al-Tirmidhi and Sunan ibn Majah. Sahih al-Bukhari and Sahih Muslim are considered to be the most reliable of these collections.

This page is intentionally left blank.

1 Introduction

Believing in all the prophets sent by Allah (God) is one of the key aspects of Islamic faith. Every Muslim, therefore, must believe in all the prophets sent by Allah (God) and His revelations. Allah says in the Quran:

Say (O Muslims), 'We believe in Allah and that which has been sent down to us and that which has been sent down to Ibrahim (Abraham), Ismail (Ishmael), Ishaq (Isaac), Yaqub (Jacob), and to Al-Asbat [the offspring of the twelve sons of Yaqub (Jacob)], and that which has been given to Musa (Moses) and Isa (Jesus), and that which has been given to the Prophets from their Lord. We make no distinction between any of them, and to Him we have submitted (in Islam) (Quran 2: 136).

One of these pious prophets was Isa (pronounced as 'Eesa') (peace be upon him) commonly referred to as 'Jesus' by Christians. Isa (Jesus) is considered to be one of the very important prophets of Islam because he was one of the four prophets to whom Allah (God) revealed His holy books. Isa (Jesus) was given the holy book named 'Injeel' (Injeel is the Quranic name of the book Bible / New Testament. However, it can't be equated fully to New Testament because Muslims consider the original revelation changed and corrupted over the years.) Allah says in the Quran:

*Then, we sent after them Our Messengers, and we
sent Isa (Jesus) - son of Maryam (Mary), and gave
him the Injeel (Gospel). And we ordained in the
hearts of those who followed him compassion
and mercy. But the monasticism which they
invented for themselves, we did not prescribe for
them, but (they sought it) only to please Allah
therewith, but they did not observe it with the
right observance. So we gave those among them
who believed their (due) reward; but many of them
are Fasiqun (rebellious, disobedient to Allah)
(Quran 57:27).*

Since his ascent to heavens, Jesus has been a subject of
debate among people from various religious backgrounds.
Many accounts of the birth, life and death of this
extraordinary man have appeared in history. Muslims believe
(according to the teachings of Quran and Prophet
Muhammad sayings) that Jesus has not died yet. Christians
believe that the stories narrated by the eight disciples of
Jesus are authentic biographical sources of Jesus' life.
However, Muslims believe that the New Testament is not a
credible source to learn about Jesus' life. According to
Islamic belief (based on Quran and Prophet Muhammad's
sayings), the originally revealed Injeel (New Testament) has
been modified (intentionally or unintentionally); therefore it
no longer remains the word of Allah.

Considering the Quran to be Allah's word, this publication
aims to present the Islamic perspective on the life of Isa or
Jesus. Furthermore, this publication will also highlight

similarities in Jesus' real teachings and the Islamic way of life (as taught by Prophet Muhammad (pbuh*).

* - "pbuh" stands for "Peace be Upon Him"

2 The Birth of Jesus

People witnessed miracles of Allah in Jesus' life right from his birth. This chapter reviews history starting from Maryam's (Mary's) birth and leading to the birth of Jesus, miracles at his birth, and how those miracles helped his mother Mary (Maryam).

2.1 Maryam's birth and her guardianship

The Quran has covered the birth of Maryam in Surah Al Imran's verse number 35 and 36. In Tafsir ibn Kathir (one of Quran's widely recognized interpretations), Ismail ibn Kathir has elaborated on these two verses and provided information about Maryam's parents. According to him, the name of Maryam's father was 'Imran'. He was an imam (prayer leader) in Bayt Al-Maqdis (Al-Aqsa site in Jerusalem that Jews refer to as the Temple Mount.) Bayt Al-Maqdis at that time was under the care of the descendents of Prophet Harun (Aron), the brother of Prophet Moosa (Moses). Imran was a very pious man and well respected by those who took care of religious affairs in Bayt Al-Maqdis. The name of Imran's wife was Hannah bint Faqudh (Hannah daughter of Faqudh) (Kathir I. , Tafsir Ibn Kathir, p. 771).

According to Ibn Kathir, Hannah didn't have any children before Maryam. One day, she saw a bird feeding its chick. Seeing that, her longing for a child grew intense and thus she made a sincere prayer to Allah (God) to grant her an offspring. In that prayer she made a promise to Allah that if He gave her an offspring, she would dedicate her child to His worship and in taking care of the holy places in Bayt Al-

Maqdis. Hannah's prayers were accepted, and soon she became pregnant. The Quran narrates her response in the following verse:

> *O my Lord! I have vowed to you what (the child that) is in my womb to be dedicated for your services (free from all worldly work; to serve Your Place of worship), so accept this from me. Verily, you are the All-Hearer, the All-Knowing (Quran 3:35).*

And after giving birth Hannah said (as narrated in the Quran):

> *Then when she gave birth to her [child Maryam (Mary)], she said: "O my Lord! I have given birth to a female child," - and Allah knew better what she brought forth, - "And the male is not like the female, and I have named her Maryam (Mary), and I seek refuge with you (Allah) for her and for her offspring from Shaitan (Satan), the outcast" (Quran 3:36).*

After the birth of Maryam, Hannah decided that she would fulfill her promise and give the newly born child to the service of Bayt-Al Maqdis. The Quran recorded this event in the following verse:

> *This is a part of the news of the Ghaib (unseen, i.e. the news of the past nations of which you have no knowledge) which We reveal to you (O Muhammad) You were not with them, when they cast lots with their pens as to which of them*

should be charged with the care of Maryam (Mary); nor were you with them when they disputed (Quran 3:44).

Ibn Kathir explains the above mentioned verse by stating the whole story in detail as described below:

Maryam's mother left with Maryam, carrying her in her infant cloth, and took her to the rabbis from the offspring of Aaron, the brother of Prophet Moses. They were responsible for taking care of Bayt Al-Maqdis (the Masjid) at that time, just as there were those who took care of the Kaabah (in Makkah). Maryam's mother said to them, "Take this child whom I vowed - to serve the Masjid, I have set her free, since she is my daughter, for no menstruating woman should enter the Masjid, and I shall not take her back home." They said, "She is the daughter of our Imam, as Imran used to lead them in prayer, "who took care of our sacrificial rituals." Zakariyya said, "Give her to me, for her maternal aunt is my wife." They said, "Our hearts cannot bear that you take her, for she is the daughter of our Imam." So they conducted a lottery with the pens with which they wrote the Tawrah, and Zakariyya won the lottery and took Maryam into his care (Kathir I. , Tafsir Ibn Kathir, p. 763).

Ibn Kathir also gives an account of the lottery as follows:

Rabbis went into the Jordan River and conducted a lottery there, deciding to throw their pens into the river. The pen that remained afloat and idle would indicate that its owner would take care of Maryam. When they threw their pens into the

6

river, the water took all the pens under, except Zakariyya's pen, which remained afloat in its place. Zakariyya was also their master, chief, scholar, Imam and Prophet, may Allah's peace and blessings are on him and the rest of the Prophets (Kathir I. , Tafsir Ibn Kathir, p. 763).

Thus, Maryam came under the guardianship of Prophet Zikariyya (Zechariah).

2.2 Life of Maryam

Maryam's guardian Zakariyya (who was the husband of Maryam's maternal aunt) was a very pious man and took good care of Maryam and raised her well. As Maryam became older, she devoted herself to the worship of Allah. Maryam fulfilled the promise of her mother and dedicated her life to the worship of Allah. She was modest, honorable, innocent, and dedicated to her task of worship.

The following hadith by Prophet Muhammad (Pbuh) shows the extent of Maryam's dedication to her worship:

The best woman (in her time) was Maryam, daughter of Imran, and the best woman (of the Prophet's time) is Khadijah (his wife), daughter of Khuwaylid (Kathir I. , Tafsir Ibn Kathir, p. 763).

Maryam's piety did not remain unobserved by Zakariyya. According to the Quran, whenever Zakariyya went to visit Maryam, he found her with food and supplies and he wondered about its source and asked her about it to which she used to respond that the food came from Allah. The Quran confirms this through the following verse:

7

So her Lord (Allah) accepted her with goodly acceptance. He made her grow in a good manner and put her under the care of Zakariyya (Zachariya). Every time he entered Al-Mihrab to (visit) her, he found her supplied with sustenance. He said: "O Maryam (Mary)! From where have you got this?" She said, "This is from Allah." Verily, Allah provides sustenance to whom He wills, without limit (Quran 3:37).

2.3 Birth of Jesus

As Maryam grew, she found out about her status of the chosen one. The Quran states:

And (remember) when the angels said: "O Maryam (Mary)! Verily, Allah has chosen you, purified you (from polytheism and disbelief), and chosen you above the women of the 'Alamin (mankind and jinn) (of her lifetime). O Mary! Submit yourself with obedience to your Lord (Allah, by worshipping none but Him Alone) and prostrate yourself, and Irkai (bow down) along with Ar-Rakiun (those who bow down) (Quran 3:42-43).

Maryam could not fully comprehend or interpret the meaning of this news. But soon she found out that she was pregnant. This astonished her because she had never been touched by a man. This obviously upset Maryam greatly and to avoid any embarrassment she withdrew from her family and the public's eye and went to a place east of Jerusalem. It was here that Allah (God) sent angel Jibrail (Gabriel) in the form of a man. This made Maryam afraid but then he gave her the news that she was about to give birth to a child named 'Isa' and that the child would be among those who are loved and blessed by Allah. Maryam was also foretold by Allah that this child would speak from his cradle. The Quran has described this instance in the following verses:

(Remember) when the angels said: "O Maryam (Mary)! Verily, Allah gives you the glad tidings of a Word ["Be!"- And he was! i.e. Isa (Jesus) the son of Maryam (Mary)] from Him, his name will be the Messiah Isa (Jesus), the son of Maryam (Mary), held in honor in this world and in the Hereafter, and will be one of those who are near to Allah. He will speak to the people in the cradle and in manhood he will be one of the righteous" (Quran 3:45-46).

In Surah Maryam, Allah describes this instance:

And mention in the Book (the Quran, O Muhammad the story of) Maryam (Mary), when she withdrew in seclusion from her family to a place facing east. She placed a screen (to screen herself) from them; then we sent to her Our Ruh [angel Jibril (Gabriel)], and he appeared before her in the form of a man in all respects. She said: "Verily! I seek refuge with the Most Gracious (Allah) from you, if you do fear Allah." (The angel) said: "I am only a messenger from your Lord, (to announce) to you the gift of a righteous son" (Quran 19: 16-19).

As is obvious, Maryam was upset to know that she was pregnant. And when the angel told her about this child she asked:

She said: "How can I have a son, when no man has touched me, nor am I unchaste?" (Quran 19:20).

Allah stated the answer of the Angel in Surah Maryam:

He said: "So (it will be), your Lord said: 'That is easy for Me (Allah): And (We wish) to appoint him as a sign to mankind and a mercy from Us (Allah), and it is a matter (already) decreed, (by Allah)'" (Quran 19:21).

Although this could have caused Maryam some agony, Allah kept her safe and filled with provisions and food. Furthermore, Allah told her not to talk to anyone about the matter and to keep quite. The Quran describes this as follows:

So she conceived him, and she withdrew with him to a far place (i.e. Bethlehem valley about 4-6 miles from Jerusalem). And the pains of childbirth drove her to the trunk of a date-palm. She said: "Would that I had died before this, and had been forgotten and out of sight!" Then [the baby Isa (Jesus) or Jibril (Gabriel)] cried unto her from below her, saying: "Grieve not: your Lord has provided a water stream under you. And shake the trunk of date-palm towards you; it will let fall fresh ripe-dates upon you. So eat and drink and be glad. And if you see any human being, say: 'Verily! I have vowed a fast unto the Most Gracious (Allah) so I shall not speak to any human being this day'" (Quran 19: 22-26).

2.4 Maryam comes back to Jerusalem

After giving birth to Prophet Isa (Jesus), Maryam came back to Jerusalem with her child. Since she was widely considered to be a pure and pious woman, the people of Jerusalem were amazed to see a child with Maryam. They asked her about his father but she said nothing and pointed to the child. This further confused the people because there was no point in asking an infant about his birth. Allah said in Surah Maryam:

> *Then she brought him (the baby) to her people, carrying him. They said: "O Mary! Indeed you have brought a thing Fariyy (a mighty thing). O sister (i.e. the like) of Harun (Aaron)! Your father was not a man who used to commit adultery, nor was your mother an unchaste woman." Then she pointed to him. They said: "How can we talk to one who is a child in the cradle?" (Quran 19: 27-29)*

In his book "Stories of Prophets", Ibn Kathir describes how Maryam came back and the Jews started asking her questions:

> *It was said that Joseph the Carpenter was greatly surprised when he knew the story, so he asked Mary: "Can a tree come to grow without a seed?" She said: "Yes, the one which Allah created for the first time." He asked her again: "Is it possible to bear a child without a male partner?" She said:*

"Yes, Allah created Adam without male or female!" (Kathir I. , Stories of Prophets, p. 178)

2.5 Jesus speaks from the cradle

While the Jews were taunting Maryam asking her about the child's father, a miracle happened. The infant which was still in cradle started speaking to the Jews. The Quran mentions the words of the infant as follows:

> *He [Isa (Jesus)] said: "Verily I am a slave of Allah, He has given me the Scripture and made me a Prophet; and He has made me blessed wheresoever's I be, and has enjoined on me Salat (prayer), and Zakat, as long as I live. And Salam (peace) be upon me the day I was born, and the day I die, and the day I shall be raised alive!" (Quran 19: 30-33)*

There is great significance to this event in Islamic history. Muhammad bin Ishaq recorded that according to Abu Hurayrah, Prophet Muhammad said:

> *No infant spoke in the cradle except Isa and the companion of Jurayj (Kathir I. , Tafsir Ibn Kathir, p. 763).*

2.6 Jews keep Jesus' miracle of speech in cradle a secret

Having witnessed this miracle, some Jews became very concerned thinking that this would impact people's beliefs.

As Ibn Kathir mentioned, the Jewish priests felt that this child could pose danger to Judaism, for they felt that the people would turn their worship to the message of Jesus (Isa) displacing the existing Jewish tenets. This would then consequently cause them to lose their authority over their people. Therefore, they kept the miracle of Jesus' speech in infancy as a secret and accused Mary of a great misdeed.

3 The Life of Jesus and his Teachings

3.1 Jesus' teachings

Muslims believe (according to the teachings of the Quran and Hadith) that Jesus (Isa) was sent to the Children of Israel by Allah because he wanted to revive the true message of Moses and all other prophets who had been sent to them before Jesus. Thus Jesus' teachings are quite similar to the commandments sent to Moses. Jesus was also sent because the Children of Israel had changed parts of Allah's message that was earlier revealed in Torah. The key to paradise according to Jesus lay in following the commandments of the one God and not to associate anyone in Allah's (God's) worship. One should note that this is the fundamental message that Muslims believe in; even the Bible relates to this message as follows:

> *Now behold, one came and said to him, "Good teacher, what good thing shall I do that I may have eternal life?" So he said to him, "Why do you call me good? No one is good but One, that is, God. But if you want to enter into life, keep the commandments" (Matthew 19:16-17).*

3.2 Similarity between Jesus' real teachings and Islamic practices

Just as Prophet Muhammad's life is an exemplary life for Muslims, Jesus' life was an example for those who followed him in his times. According to John:

> *Jesus said to him, "I am the way, and the truth and the life; no one comes to Father but to me" (John 14:6).*

This verse is commonly quoted by Christians to prove the divinity of Jesus. But some would interpret to say that if anyone wants to worship God he must follow the ways of Jesus. The same has also been said to Prophet Muhammad by Allah in Surah AL-Imran. Allah says in the Quran:

> *Say (O Muhammad to mankind): "If you (really) love Allah then follow me (i.e. accept Islamic Monotheism, follow the Quran and the Sunnah), Allah will love you and forgive you your sins. And Allah is Oft-Forgiving, Most Merciful." (Quran 3:31).*

One of the main objectives of Allah's prophets was to convey Allah's teachings to people. Additionally, prophets were also sent to set an example and be role models for people to follow. All prophets thus taught their people about worshipping Allah the way Allah wanted it. Any deviations from that message thus constitutes as innovation in Islam. To this, Prophet Muhammad said:

Whoever adds anything new to the religion of Islam will have it rejected [by God] (Hadith Bukhari, Vol. 3, p.535, no.861).

As it has been mentioned before, Jesus was the last among the Jewish Prophets and he was sent to revive the true and lost message of Torah. Jesus did not give any new instructions to the Children of Israel; his aim was not to abolish the law but to fulfill it.

Dr Bilal Philips (an Islamic scholar) has identified certain practices of Jesus which establish the similarity between Christian practices and those practices that were taught by Prophet Muhammad to the followers of Islam. Although according to Muslims, the message of the original Bible was changed with the passage of time, one can still find many messages in the Bible that mirror certain Islamic teachings. The following sections highlight some of those teachings.

3.2.1 Circumcision

As mentioned before, Jesus came to the world to uphold what had been told to earlier prophets. One of the instructions that were given to prophets was about circumcision. Allah said to Abraham in the Old Testament:

This is my covenant, which ye shall keep, between me and you and thy seed after thee; every man child among you shall be circumcised. And ye shall circumcise the flesh of your foreskin; and it shall be a token of the covenant betwixt me and you. And he that is eight days old shall be

> *circumcised among you, every man child in your generations, he that is born in the house, or bought with money of any stranger, which is not of thy seed. He that is born in thy house, and he that is bought with thy money, needs be circumcised: and my covenant shall be in your flesh for an everlasting covenant (Genesis 17:10-13).*

Just as Allah had commanded, Jesus was also circumcised in flesh. Luke recorded this event in the following words:

> *And at the end of eight days, when he was circumcised, he was called Jesus, the name given by the angel before he was conceived in the womb (Luke 2:21).*

Hence, it's clear from the Bible that Jesus was circumcised. But a number of today's Christians do not believe in this as a commandment because Paul later instructed them that Jesus was circumcised from the heart. He said:

> *He is a Jew who is one inwardly, and real circumcision is the matter of heart, spiritual and not literal (Romans 2:29).*

In fact Paul's interpretation is inconsistent with the Old Testament, which clearly stated that a male should be circumcised in flesh rather than heart. Prophet Muhammad (pbuh) also emphasized the importance of this tradition by saying:

There are five practices which constitute the prophetic way: circumcision, shaving pubic hair and underarm hair, clipping fingernails and toenails; trimming the moustache (Sahih Bukhari, vol. 7, p.515).

3.2.2 Prohibition of eating pork

Another difference between Muslims and Christians is that Christians eat pork whereas Muslims are prohibited from eating it. Careful reading of Bible reveals that Jesus did not eat pork and he strictly forbade that to his followers as well.

And the swine, it parts the hoof and is cloven footed but does not chew the cud, is unclean for you. Of their flesh you shall not eat, and their carcasses you shall not touch: they are unclean for you (Leviticus 11:7-8).

Similar to Jesus' teaching, Allah has prohibited pork for Muslims. In the Quran Allah says:

He has forbidden you only the Maitah (dead animals), and blood, and the flesh of swine, and that which is slaughtered as a sacrifice for others than Allah (or has been slaughtered for idols, on which Allah's Name has not been mentioned while slaughtering). But if one is forced by necessity without willful disobedience nor transgressing due limits, then there is no sin on him. Truly, Allah is Oft-Forgiving, Most Merciful (Quran 2:173).

3.2.3 Proper animals slaughter methods

Jesus ate only the flesh of those animals which had been properly slaughtered. If the flesh of any slaughtered animal contained blood in it Jesus did not eat it. The Old Testament says:

> *Only you shall not eat blood; you shall pour it upon the earth like water (Deuteronomy 12:16).*

> *You shall not eat any flesh with blood in it. You shall not practice augury or witchcraft (Levictus 19: 26).*

Islamic way of slaughtering entails that the animal is slaughtered at the throat severing the key arteries and veins that in turn forces all the blood out of the animal's body. Jewish religious law advocated the same practices as it clears the animal's organs from blood.

Today, most Christians eat meat that doesn't conform to these practices leaving the blood within the meat of the animal. Allah states in the Quran:

> *Say (O Muhammad): "I find not in that which has been revealed to me anything forbidden to be eaten by one who wishes to eat it, unless it be Maitah (a dead animal) or blood poured forth (by slaughtering or the like), or the flesh of swine (pork); for that surely is impure or impious*

(unlawful) meat (of an animal) which is slaughtered as a sacrifice for others than Allah (or has been slaughtered for idols, or on which Allah's Name has not been mentioned while slaughtering). But whosoever is forced by necessity without willful disobedience, nor transgressing due limits; (for him) certainly, your Lord is Oft-Forgiving, Most Merciful" (Quran 6:145).

And for every nation we have appointed religious ceremonies, that they may mention the Name of Allah over the beast of cattle that He has given them for food. And your Ilah (God) is One Ilah (God - Allah), so you must submit to Him Alone (in Islam). And (O Muhammad) give glad tidings to the Mukhbitin (those who obey Allah with humility and are humble from among the true believers of Islamic Monotheism) (Quran 22: 34).

3.2.4 Prohibition of Alcohol

Like Muslims, Jesus abstained himself from alcohol and taught his followers to stay away from this evil too. According to the Old Testament:

And the Lord said to Moses, "Say to the people of Israel, When either a man or a woman makes a special vow, the vow of the Nazairite, to separate himself to the lord, he shall separate himself from wine and strong drink: he shall drink no vinegar made from wine or strong drink, and shall not drink any juice of grapes or eat grapes, fresh or died. All day of his separation he shall eat nothing that is produced by the grapevine, not even the seeds or skins" (Number 6:1-4).

As has been mentioned before, Jesus followed Mosaic Law and, therefore, it can be concluded that Jesus did not drink wine.

Islamic teachings strongly warn Muslims to stay away from alcoholic drinks. Allah states in the Quran:

O you who believe! Intoxicants (all kinds of alcoholic drinks), and gambling, and Al-Ansab, and Al-Azlam (arrows for seeking luck or decision) are an abomination of Shaitan's (Satan) handiwork. So avoid (strictly all) that (abomination) in order that you may be successful (Quran 5:90).

Christians might use the argument that one of Jesus' miracles was turning water into wine. However, if wine was forbidden in Christianity, then one would argue the validity of those facts. Dr. Bilal Philips responds to this in the article "The True Message of Jesus Christ" where he says:

... the miracle of turning water into wine, it is found only in Gospel of John, which consistently contradicts the other three Gospels . . . The Gospel of John was opposed as heretical in the early church, while the other three Gospels were referred to as synoptic Gospels because text contained a similar treatment of Jesus' life.

Consequently, New Testament scholars have expressed doubt about the authenticity of this incident (Philips, 1996, p. 84).

3.2.5 Ablution before prayer

In following Moses' religion, Jesus must have performed ablution before saying formal prayers as the Old Testament says:

And he set the Lever between tent of the meeting and the Altar, and put water in it for washing. With which Moses and Aron and his sons washed their hands and their feet. As the Lord commanded Moses (Exodus 40:30-31).

Muslims perform ablution (washing) before saying formal prayers. Allah says in the Quran:

O you who believe! When you intend to offer As-Salat (the prayer), wash your faces and your hands (forearms) up to the elbows, rub (by passing wet hands over) your heads, and (wash) your feet up to ankles. If you are in a state of Janaba (i.e. after a sexual discharge), purify yourselves (bathe your whole body). But if you are ill or on a journey, or any of you comes after answering the call of nature, or you have been in contact with women (i.e. sexual intercourse), and you find no water, then perform Tayammum with clean earth and rub therewith your faces and hands. Allah does not want to place you in difficulty, but He wants to purify you, and to complete His Favor to you that you may be thankful (Quran 5:6).

3.2.6 Prostration in prayer

Similar to Islamic worship practices, Jesus is also known to have prostrated during his prayers. Matthew states:

> *And going a little further he fell on his face and prayed, "My Father, if it be possible, let this cup from me; nevertheless, not as I will, but as thou wilt" (Matthew 26:39).*

Christians of today kneel down, but they do not exactly follow what Jesus did, that is, fell on his face (referred to as prostration or "sajda" in Arabic). Other prophets before Jesus too were ordered to prostrate properly in front of Allah.

> *Abraham fell face down, and God said to him . . . (Genesis 17:3).*

> *But Moses and Aaron fell face down and cried out, "O God, God of the spirits of all mankind, will you be angry with the entire assembly when only one man sins?" (Numbers 16:22).*

> *"Neither," he replied, "but as commander of the army of the LORD I have now come." Then Joshua fell face down to the ground in reverence,*

and asked him, *"What message does my Lord have for his servant?" (Joshua 5:14)*

In the Quran, Allah has instructed Muslims to prostrate to Him. Allah states in the Quran:

And during night, prostrate yourself to Him (i.e. the offering of Maghrib and 'Isha' prayers), and glorify Him a long night through (i.e. Tahajjud prayer) (Quran 76: 26).

3.2.7 Commandments for Veiling and Covering

Similar to Muslim women of today, early followers of Jesus also observed modesty in their attire including covering heads from strangers. During those times, it was a general custom among Jews to wear the veil. The Old Testament states:

And Rabekha lifted her eyes, and when she saw Isaac, she alighted from the camel, and said to the servant. "Who is the man yonder, walking in the field to meet us?" The servant said, "it is my master." So she took her veil and covered herself (Genesis 24:64-65).

Even Paul emphasized the importance of the veil when he said:

But any woman who prays or prophesies with her head unveiled dishonors her head—it is the same as if her head were shaven. For if a woman will not veil herself, then she would cut off her hair; but if it is disgraceful for a woman to be shorn or shaven, let her wear a veil (Coronthian 11: 5-6).

Muslim women are also instructed to cover for modesty as is known by the Islamic teachings related to wearing of the Hijab and the Jilbab (Abaya). The Quran states:

And tell the believing women to lower their gaze (from looking at forbidden things), and protect their private parts (from illegal sexual acts) and not to show off their adornment except only that which is apparent and to draw their veils all over Juyubihinna (i.e. their bodies, faces, necks and bosoms) and not to reveal their adornment except to their husbands, or their fathers, or their husband's fathers, or their sons, or their husband's sons, or their brothers or their brother's sons, or their sister's sons, or their (Muslim) women (i.e. their sisters in Islam), or the (female) slaves whom their right hands possess, or old male servants who lack vigour, or small children who have no sense of feminine sex. And let them not stamp their feet so as to reveal what they hide of their adornment. And all of you beg Allah to forgive you all, O believers, that you may be successful (Quran 24:31).

O Prophet! Tell your wives and your daughters and the women of the believers to draw their cloaks (veils) all over their bodies. That will be better, that they should be known (as free respectable women) so as not to be annoyed. And Allah is ever Oft-Forgiving, Most Merciful (Quran 33:59).

3.2.8 Fasting

Fasting is also one of the acts of worship that is common between Islamic and Jesus' early teachings. According to Matthew Jesus fasted for forty days.

And he fasted forty days and forty nights, and afterwards he was hungry (Matthew 4:2).

Fasting was also performed by many prophets before Jesus. Prophet Moses also fasted for forty days:

And he was there with the lord, for forty days and forty nights; he neither ate bread nor drank water; and he wrote upon tables, the words of the covenants, the Ten Commandments (Exodus 34:28).

Similarly, Muslims have also been instructed to keep the fast. Allah said in the Quran:

O you who believe! Observing As-Saum (the fasting) is prescribed for you as it was prescribed for those before you, that you may become Al-Muttaqun (Quran 2:183).

3.2.9 Prohibition of Interest

Another similarity between Jesus, the Mosaic law (Law of Moses) and the law revealed to Prophet Muhammad (pbuh) is that all condemned the practice of taking interest. The Mosaic Law states:

> *You shall not lend upon interest to your brother, interest on money, interest upon victuals, interest on anything that is lent for interest (Deuteronomy 23:19).*

Similarly Allah has forbidden interest to Muslims. Allah says in the Quran:

> *O you who believe! Be afraid of Allah and give up what remains (due to you) from Riba (usury) (from now onward), if you are (really) believers (Quran 2:278).*

3.2.10 Disparaging of pagan practices

Jesus forbade all pagan practices of his time. Those included worshipping of many gods instead of the one true God and making images of what was thought to be in the heavens. The logic behind the forbidding of making images of heavenly objects was that these images limit God's created beauty to only what a human mind can conceive. In fact a human mind is simply incapable of imagining God's greatness.

Jesus upheld the prohibition mentioned in Torah:

You shall not make for yourself a graven image, or any likeness of anything that is in heaven above, or that is in the earth beneath, or that is in the water under the earth (Exodus 20: 4).

The Quran states:

".......So shun the abomination (worshipping) of idol, and shun lying speech (false statements)" Quran (22:30)

"And the people of Moosa (Moses) made in his absence, out of their ornaments, the image of a calf (for worship). It had a sound (as if it was mooing). Did they not see that it could neither speak to them nor guide them to the way? They took it for worship and they were Zalimoon (wrong-doers)". Quran (7:148)

3.3 Stories from Jesus' life

Just like his birth, Jesus' life was also extraordinary. Ibn Kathir has quoted some stories from Jesus' life. The following story quoted from Ibn Kathir's book provides an insight into Jesus' life and how he rebelled against the false practices of the (Jewish) people of his time:

As Jesus (pbuh) grew, the signs of prophet hood began to increase. He could tell his friends what kind of supper waited for them at home and what they had hidden and where. When he was twelve years old, he accompanied his mother to Jerusalem. There he wandered into the temple and joined a crowd listening to the lecture of the Rabbis (Jewish priests). The audience was all adults, but he was not afraid to sit with them. After listening intently, he asked questions and expressed his opinion. The learned rabbis were disturbed by the boy's boldness and puzzled by the questions he asked, for they were unable to answer him. They tried to silence him, but he ignored their attempts and continued to express his views. Jesus became so involved in this exchange that he forgot he was expected back home.

In the meantime, his mother went home, thinking that he might have gone back with relatives or friends. When she arrived, she discovered that he was not there, so she returned to the city to look for him. At last she found him in the temple, sitting among the learned, conversing with them. He appeared to be quite at ease, as if he had been doing this all his life. Mary got angry with him for causing her worry. He tried to assure her that all the arguing and debating with the learned had made him forget the time.

Jesus grew up to manhood. It was Sabbath, a day of complete rest: no fire could be lit or extinguished nor could females plait their hair. Moses (pbuh) had commanded that Saturday be dedicated to the worship of Allah. However, the wisdom behind the Sabbath and its spirit had gone, and only the letter remained in the Jews' hearts. Also, they thought that Sabbath was kept in heaven, and that the People of Israel had been chosen by Allah only to observe the Sabbath."

Ibn Kathir further writes:

"Jesus was on his way to the temple. Although it was the Sabbath, he reached out his hand to pick two pieces of fruit to feed a hungry child. This was considered to be a violation of the Sabbath law. He made a fire for the old women to keep themselves warm from the freezing air. He went to the temple and looked around. There were twenty thousand Jewish priests registered there who earned their living from the temple. The rooms of the temple were full of them.

Jesus observed that the visitors were much fewer than the priests. Yet the temple was full of sheep and doves which were sold to the people to be offered as sacrifices. Every step in the temple cost the visitor money. They worshipped nothing but money. In the temple, the Pharisees and Sadducees acted as if it was a market place, and these two groups always disagreed on everything. Jesus followed the scene with his eyes and observed that the poor people who could not afford the price of the sheep or dove were swept away like flies by the Pharisees and Sadducees. Jesus was astonished. Why did the priests burn a lot of offerings inside the temple, while thousands of poor people were hungry outside it?

On this blessed night, the two noble prophets John (Yahya in Islam) (pbuh) and Zakariyya (pbuh) died, killed by the ruling authority. On the same night, the revelation descended upon Jesus (pbuh). Allah the Exalted commanded him to begin his call to the children of Israel. To Jesus, the life of ease was closed, and the page of worship and struggle was opened.

Like an opposing force, the message of Jesus came to denounce the practices of the Pharisees and to reinforce the Law of Moses. In the face of a materialistic age of luxury and worship of gold, Jesus called his people to a nobler life by word and deed. This exemplary life was the only way out of the wretchedness and diseases of his age. Jesus' call, from the beginning, was marked by its complete uprightness and piety. It appealed to the soul, the inner being, and not be a closed system of rules laid down by society (Kathir I. , Stories of Prophets, pp. 178-180).

3.4 Jesus was an ethnic Prophet

An ethnic prophet is the one who is sent to a particular ethnicity and whose aim is to guide that particular ethnicity to Allah's righteous path. Prophets sent to the Children of Israel were such prophets because all of them came to guide that specific nation. Since Jesus came to the Children of Israel, it is often argued that he came just to guide the Children of Israel and not the whole of mankind. As Bible states:

I was not sent except to the lost sheep of the house of Israel. Do not go into the way of Gentiles, and do not enter a city of Samaritans, but go rather to the lost sheep of the house of Israel (Matthew 10: 5-6).

In the above mentioned verse the word "gentile" refers to non-Israelites. Hence, one can say that Jesus did not come to the whole of mankind, but rather he came for a particular group of people called the Children of Israel. This is unlike Prophet Muhammad (pbuh) who, according to Islamic beliefs, came to guide the entire humanity – not any specific ethnicity. Allah has clearly indicated this in various verses of the Quran.

And We have not sent you (O Muhammad) except as a giver of glad tidings and a warner to all mankind, but most of men know not. (Quran 34:28)

O mankind! Verily, there has come to you the Messenger (Muhammad) with the truth from your Lord, so believe in him, it is better for you. But if you disbelieve, then certainly to Allah belongs all that is in the heavens and the earth. And Allah is Ever AllKnowing, AllWise. (Quran 4:170)

O people of the Scripture (Jews and Christians)! Do not exceed the limits in your religion, nor say of Allah aught but the truth. The Messiah Iesa (Jesus), son of Maryam (Mary), was (no more than) a Messenger of Allah and His Word, ("Be!" - and he was) which He bestowed on Maryam (Mary) and a spirit (Rooh) created by Him; so believe in Allah and His Messengers. Say not: "Three (trinity)!" Cease! (it is) better for you. For Allah is (the only) One Ilah (God), Glory be to Him (Far Exalted is He) above having a son. To Him belongs all that is in the heavens and all that is in the earth. And Allah is All Sufficient as a Disposer of affairs. (Quran 4:171)

4   Miracles of Jesus

There are many verses in Quran which discuss the miracles performed by Jesus. Allah says in Quran;

> *"...and we made her (Mary) and her son (Jesus) a sign for the worlds." (Quran 21:91)*

At another place in Quran, Allah says;

> *"...And We gave Iesa (Jesus), the son of Maryam (Mary), clear signs and supported him with Rooh-ul-Qudus (Jibrael (Gabriel))...." (Quran 2:87)*

Apart from the above mentioned miraculous birth of Jesus without a father, Quran has mentioned the following miracles of Jesus:

1. He spoke as an infant in the cradle.
2. Allah sent a table of food for his disciples on his request.
3. He could breathe life into objects made of clay.
4. He could heal the blind and lepers.
5. He was given the power to know what people had eaten and stored in their homes.

These miracles are described in the following passages.

4.1 Jesus speaking in the cradle as an infant

As mentioned earlier, Jesus spoke from his cradle to justify the innocence of his mother Maryam. Allah foretold Maryam about this miracle.

> *"He will speak to the people in the cradle and in manhood, and he will be one of the righteous."*
> *(Quran 3:46)*

4.2 Allah sent a table of food for his disciples on his request

The fifth chapter of Quran has been named after one of the miracles of Jesus. The name of this chapter is "Surah Al-Māʾidah." English translation of the word "Al-Maʾidah" is "The Table Spread". The name of this surah (chapter) refers to an incident where Jesus' disciples asked him to request Allah for a table laden with food. When Jesus asked them why they wanted such a table, they answered that it would fulfill their need for food and it will make them first hand witnesses of a miracle. Therefore, this table would strengthen their belief and make them worship more. Quran describes this incident in the following words:

> *(Remember) when Al-Hawareeoon (the disciples) said: "O Iesa (Jesus), son of Maryam (Mary)! Can your Lord send down to us a table spread (with food) from heaven?" Iesa (Jesus) said: "Fear Allah, if you are indeed believers."*
>
> *They said: "We wish to eat thereof and to be stronger in Faith, and to know that you have indeed told us the truth and that we ourselves be its witnesses."*

Iesa (Jesus), son of Maryam (Mary), said: "O Allah, our Lord! Send us from heaven a table spread (with food) that there may be for us - for the first and the last of us - a festival and a sign from You; and provide us sustenance, for You are the Best of sustainers." Quran (5:112-114)

On the request of Jesus therefore Allah granted such a table to the disciples of Jesus. But this favor by Allah was not unconditional. Allah said to the disciples that he would grant them such a table on Jesus' request but if anyone among them disbelieved after that then his punishment would be the severest of all.

"Allah said: "I am going to send it down unto you, but if any of you after that disbelieves, then I will punish him with a torment such as I have not inflicted on anyone among (all) the 'Alamin (mankind and jinn)." (Quran 5:115)

Ibn-e-Kathir recorded from ibn-e-Jarir's writings that Ishaq bin `Abdullah said, "...the table was sent down to `Isa son of Maryam having seven pieces of bread and seven fish, and they ate from it as much as they wished. But when some of them stole food from it, saying, *'It might not come down tomorrow,' the table ascended."*

Ibn Kathir writes about this incident in his book, Qasas-ul-Anbiyaa (Stories of the Prophets):

"It was related that Jesus commanded his disciples to fast for thirty days; at the end of it, they asked Jesus to bring food from heaven to

break their fast. Jesus prayed to Allah after his disciples had doubted Allah's power. The great table came down between two clouds, one above and one below, while the people watched. Jesus said: "O Lord, make it a mercy and not a cause of distress." So it fell between Jesus' hands, covered with a napkin.

Jesus suddenly prostrated and his disciples with him. They sensed a fragrance, which they had never smelled before. Jesus said: "The one who is the most devout and most righteous may uncover the table, that we might eat of it to thank Allah for it." They said: "O Spirit of Allah, you are the most deserving."

Jesus stood up, then performed ablution and prayed before uncovering the table, and behold, there was a roasted fish. The disciples said: "O Spirit of Allah, is this the food of this world or of Paradise?" Jesus said to his disciples: "Did not Allah forbid you to ask questions? It is the divine power of Allah the Almighty who said: 'Be,' and it was. It is a sign from Almighty Allah warning of great punishment for unbelieving mortals of the world. This is the kernel of the matter."

It is said that thousands of people partook of it, and yet they never exhausted it. A further miracle was that the blind and lepers were cured.

The Day of the Table became one of the holy days for the disciples and followers of Jesus. Later on, the disciples and followers forgot the real essence of the miracles, and so they worshipped Jesus as a god" (Kathir I. , Stories of Prophets, p. 179)

4.3 Jesus could breathe life into objects made of clay

Just as Allah made Adam out of clay and then breathed life into him, Allah had empowered Jesus with the miraculous power to breathe life into birds made of clay. But this again does not mean that Quran intended to say that Jesus was "Godly". According to Quran, Jesus was a prophet and all his miracles were given to him by Allah. According to Quran Jesus said to Israelites:

> *And will make him (Iesa (Jesus)) a Messenger to the Children of Israel (saying): "I have come to you with a sign from your Lord, that I design for you out of clay, as it were, the figure of a bird, and breathe into it, and it becomes a bird by Allah's Leave; and I heal him who was born blind, and the leper, and I bring the dead to life by Allah's Leave. And I inform you of what you eat, and what you store in your houses. Surely, therein is a sign for you, if you believe. (Quran 3:49)*

4.4 Healing the Blind and the Leper

Just like the New Testament, Quran also testifies that Jesus had the power to heal. His power to heal was so profound that he could even heal those which were impossible to heal through medicine such as blind and lepers.

> *And will make him (Iesa (Jesus)) a Messenger to the Children of Israel (saying): "I have come to you with a sign from your Lord, that I design for*

37

you out of clay, as it were, the figure of a bird, and breathe into it, and it becomes a bird by Allahs Leave; and I heal him who was born blind, and the leper, and I bring the dead to life by Allahs Leave. And I inform you of what you eat, and what you store in your houses. Surely, therein is a sign for you, if you believe. (Quran 3:49)

In this verse, Quran has used the word "Akmah" for blind which translates into English as "A person who is born blind". This means that Jesus could even cure those who were born blind. This does not stop here, Jesus was granted the power to even resurrect the dead from their graves but this was all done by the permission of Allah.

"...and I bring the dead to life, by Allah's Leave (by the permission of God.)" (Quran 3:49)

Ibn kathir states in Qasas-ul-Anbiya:

"Jesus continued his mission, aided by divine miracles. Some Quranic commentators said that Jesus brought four people back from the dead: a friend of his named Al-Azam, an old woman's son, and a woman's only daughter. These three had died during his lifetime. When the Jews saw this they said: "You only resurrect those who have died recently; perhaps they only fainted." They asked him to bring back to life Sam the Ibn Noah (Noah's son).

When he asked them to show him his grave, the people accompanied him there. Jesus invoked Allah the Exalted to bring him back to life and behold, Sam the Ibn Noah came out from the grave gray-haired. Jesus asked: "how did you get gray hair, when there was no aging in your time?"

He answered: "O Spirit of Allah, I thought that the Day of Resurrection had come; from the fear of that day my hair turned gray." (Kathir I. , Stories of Prophets, p. 180)

4.5 Power to know what people had eaten and stored in their homes

Another miracle possessed by Jesus was his power to know what people had eaten and what they had stored in their homes.

".........I (Jesus) inform you too of what things you eat, and what you store up in your houses. Surely in that is a sign for you, if you are believers." (Quran 3:49)

5 Islamic explanation refuting Jesus as being son of God

Allah has clearly stated the miracle of the birth of Jesus in the Quran. Contrary to the teachings of the Quran, Christians believe that Jesus (Isa) was the son of Allah. According to the Quran, Jesus had no father. His birth was a miracle of God (Allah). The Quran states:

> *"And they (Jews, Christians and pagans) say: Allah has begotten a son (Children or offspring). Glory be to Him (Exalted be He above all that they associate with Him). Nay, to Him belongs all that is in the heavens and on earth, and all surrender with obedience (in worship) to Him, The Originator of the heavens and the earth. When He decrees a matter, He only says to it: "Be!" and it is" (Quran 2:116-17).*

Wherever Allah mentioned the name of Jesus in the Quran, He referred to him as "Isa-ibn-Maryam" (Isa or Jesus the son of Maryam). According to the Quran, it does not befit Allah's majesty to have a son. Allah says in the Quran:

> *"It befits not (the Majesty of) Allah that He should beget a son [this refers to the slander of Christians against Allah, by saying that 'Îsa (Jesus) is the son of Allah]. Glorified (and Exalted) be He (above all that they associate with Him). When He decrees a thing, He only says to it: "Be!" - and it is (Quran 19: 35).*

Allah then refers to those who call Jesus as son of God, i.e., Christians, and states the following:

> *And they say: The Most Gracious (Allah) has begotten a son (or offspring or children) [as the Jews say: 'Uzair (Ezra) is the son of Allah, and the Christians say that He has begotten a son ['Îsa (Jesus)], and the pagan Arabs say that He has begotten daughters (angels and others.)]. Indeed you have brought forth (said) a terrible evil thing. Whereby the heavens are almost torn, and the earth is split asunder, and the mountains fall in ruins, That they ascribe a son (or offspring or children) to the Most Gracious (Allah). But it is not suitable for (the Majesty of) the Most Gracious (Allah) that He should beget a son (or offspring or children). There is none in the heavens and the earth but comes unto the Most Gracious (Allah) as a slave (Quran 19: 88-93).*

> *Verily! This is the true narrative [about the story of 'Îsa (Jesus)], and La ilaha illallah (none has the right to be worshipped but Allah, the One and the Only True God, Who has neither a wife nor a son). And indeed, Allah is the All-Mighty, the All-Wise (Quran 3:62).*

On the topic of the uniqueness of Allah (God), the Quran states the following:

> *Say (O Muhammad (Peace be upon him)): He is Allah, (the) One.*

> *Allah-us-Samad (The Self-Sufficient Master, Whom all creatures need, He neither eats nor drinks).*

> *He begets not, nor was He begotten;*

And there is none co-equal or comparable unto Him.

-- (Quran 112:1-4)

As mentioned earlier, the Quran fully recognizes that Jesus did not have a father; nor was he born with the aid of any human. According to Ibn Kathir, if Allah had to have a son it would more likely be Adam because Adam had no one before him. But since it does not befit Allah to have a son neither Adam nor Jesus is the son of Allah. According to the Quran both Adam and Jesus came into the world as miracles of Allah. The Quran states:

Verily, the likeness of Isa (Jesus) before Allah is the likeness of Adam. He created him from dust, then (He) said to him: "Be!" - and he was (Quran 3:59).

5.1 Misinterpretations about 'son of God'

Even if one has to accept that there are passages in the Bible where Jesus has been called the son of God, there are also other explanations that contradict this notion. One such explanation has been provided by Bilal Philips in his book *"The True Message of Jesus Christ."* He has identified many places in the Hebrew Bible where God has called other prophets as his sons, but no one considered those prophets to be literally God's sons. It was because in Hebrew tradition, the term "God's son" does not literally mean the son of the Almighty. This term has to be understood in a metaphorical sense. The term "God's son" means the follower of the path that has been declared righteous by God. According to Bilal, Christians detached themselves from the Hebrew tradition when they started taking the term "God's son" in its literal sense.

As mentioned above, Bilal has identified many passages in sacred Hebrew texts where God has referred to his prophets as his sons, but not in a literal sense. According to Bilal:

> *God called Israel (Prophet Jacob) His "son" when He instructed Prophet Moses to go to Pharaoh in Exodus 4:22-23: 22: And you shall say to Pharaoh, 'Thus says the Lord, "Israel is my first-born son, and I say to you, 'Let my son go that he may serve me.' (See also, Hosea 1:10, of the King James Version.) In 2nd Samuel 8:13-14, God calls Prophet Solomon His son: 13: He [Solomon] shall build a house for my name, and I will establish the throne of his kingdom forever. 14: I will be his father, and he shall be my son. God promised to make Prophet David His son in Psalms 89:26-27: 26 He shall cry unto me, "Thou art my father, my God, and the rock of my salvation, 27Also I will make him my first-born, higher than the kings of the earth." (In the Revised Standard Version, it states: "And I will make him the first-born, the highest of the kings of the earth." See also Jeremiah 31:9: ". . . for I am a father to Israel and Ephraim is my first-born." Angels are referred to as "sons of God" in The Book of Job 1:6: Now there was a day when the sons of God came to present themselves before the Lord, and Satan also came among them. (See also, Job 2:1 and 38:4-7. Other references to sons of God can also be found in Genesis 6:2, Deuteronomy 14:1 and Hosea 1:10.) In the New Testament, there are many references to "sons of God" other than Jesus. For example,*

when the author of the Gospel according to Luke listed Jesus' ancestors back to Adam, he wrote: "The son of Enos, the son of Seth, the son of Adam, the son of God."

It is also argued by some that Jesus was the begotten son of God and others were not. However, there are passages in Hebrew Bible where others have been referred to as begotten sons of God. For example, God said to David, "I will tell the decree of the Lord." He said to me, "You are my son, today I have taken so. Begotten you" (Psalms 2:7).

<u>Since none of these literally mean that someone is the son of God therefore it should be understood that Jesus was not literally the son of God. This term has metaphorical meaning and it has to be</u> (Philips, 1996, pp. 46-48).

Bilal goes further to conclude that the term "son of God" is not to be taken in its literal sense:

Since the Hebrews believed that God is One, and had neither wife nor children in any literal sense, it is obvious that the expression "son of God" merely meant to them "Servant of God"; one who, because of his faithful service, was close and dear to God, as a son is to a father. Christians who came from a Greek or Roman background later misused this term. In their heritage, "son of God" signified an incarnation of a god or someone born of a physical union between male and female gods. When the Church cast aside its Hebrew foundations, it adopted the pagan concept of "son of God," which was entirely *different from the Hebrew usage. <u>Consequently, the use of the term "son of God" should only be understood from the Semitic symbolic sense of a "servant of God," and not in the pagan sense of a literal offspring of God.</u> In the four Gospels, Jesus is recorded as saying: "Blessed are the peacemakers; they will be called sons of God"* (Philips, 1996, p. 49).

Moreover, there are many places in the Bible where Jesus has referred to himself as a son of man rather than a son of God. For example:

And he said, "The Son of Man must suffer many things and be rejected by the elders, chief priests and teachers of the law, and he must be killed and on the third day be raised to life" (Luke 9:22).

There are also passages in the Bible where Jesus rejected being called the son of God. For example:

Moreover, demons came out of many people, shouting, "You are the Son of God!" But he rebuked them and would not allow them to speak, because they knew he was the Christ" (Luke 4:41).

Some Christians provide the following passage as a proof to show that Jesus literally considered himself the son of God. When Jesus was asked by his followers to show the father he said:

Do you not believe that I am in the Father and the father is in me? The word that I say to you I do not say on my own authority; but the father who dwells in me does his works. Believe me that father is in me and I am in the father; or else believe me for the sake of the works themselves (John 14: 10-11).

However, these Christians ignore the fact that within the Bible itself Jesus said the following just nine verses later:

In that day you will know that I am in my father and you are in me and I in you (John 14:20).

Taken from a Christian perspective, if both of these verses are taken literally, then it would be true to say that Jesus was the son of God. However, in that case it would also be equally true to say that the disciples were also God because the second verse literally says so. Thus, it becomes clear from these two verses that none of them has to be taken literally. Contrary to the literal meaning, oneness does not mean oneness of essence. It means oneness of purpose.

According to the Bible, Jesus, at the end of his mission, made it clear that God is not only his father, but the father of all, and God of all, and even his own God. Assuming that's true (father of all), that would have been true for everyone – not just Jesus. He said:

I am ascending to my Father and your Father, to my God and your God (John 20: 17).

Thus, such misinterpretations from the life of Jesus in the early periods resulted in laying the foundation of erroneous beliefs.

5.2 Quran's rejection of the notion of God's son

The Quran has totally rejected the notion that Jesus was the son of Allah. According to the Quran, having a son does not befit Allah's greatness. According to the Quran, Jesus was a prophet of Allah who was sent to the Children of Israel to revive the commandments that were given to Moses. Allah says in the Quran:

> *The Messiah ['Îsa (Jesus)], son of Maryam (Mary), was no more than a Messenger; many were the Messengers that passed away before him. His mother [Maryam (Mary)] was a Siddiqah [i.e. she believed in the Words of Allah and His Books (see Verse 66:12)]. They both used to eat food (as any other human being, while Allah does not eat). Look how We make the Ayat (proofs, evidence, verses, lessons, signs, revelations, etc.) clear to them; yet look how they are deluded away (from the truth) (Quran 5:75).*

In the following verse, we can see that Allah will ask Jesus on the day of resurrection whether he claimed deity or not. In answer to that Jesus (Isa) will clearly say that he never claimed to be more than a prophet. The Quran states:

And (remember) when Allah will say (on the Day of Resurrection): "O 'Īsa (Jesus), son of Maryam (Mary)! Did you say unto men: 'Worship me and my mother as two gods besides Allah?'" He will say: "Glory be to You! It was not for me to say what I had no right (to say). Had I said such a thing, you would surely have known it. You know what is in my inner-self though I do not know what is in Yours; truly, You, only You, are the All-Knower of all that is hidden (and unseen). Never did I say to them aught except what you (Allah) did command me to say: 'Worship Allah, my Lord and your Lord.' And I was a witness over them while I dwelt amongst them, but when you took me up, You were the Watcher over them; and You are a Witness to all things. (This is a great admonition and warning to the Christians of the whole world). If you punish them, they are Your slaves, and if You forgive them, verily You, only You, are the All-Mighty, the All-Wise" (Quran 5: 116-118).

6 Islamic views on the disciples of Jesus

Every prophet had his own disciples. According to one Hadith,

"It is narrated on the authority of 'Abdullah ibn Mas'ud that the Messenger of Allah (Prophet Muhammad) (May peace and blessings be upon him) observed:

> *Never a Prophet had been sent before me by Allah towards his nation who had not among his people (his) disciples and companions who followed his ways and obeyed his command. Then there came after them their successors who said whatever they did not practice, and practiced whatever they were not commanded to do. He who strove against them with his hand was a believer: he who strove against them with his tongue was a believer, and he who strove against them with his heart was a believer and beyond that there is no faith even to the extent of a mustard seed (Sahih Muslim; vol. 1; ch 21).*

In order to help Jesus in spreading the message of truth, Allah also gave him disciples like all other prophets. Although their names and identities are not mentioned in the Quran, their references are very explicit:

> *And will make him [(Isa (Jesus)] a Messenger to the Children of Israel (saying): "I have come to you with a sign from your Lord, that I design for you out of clay, a figure like that of a bird, and breathe into it, and it becomes a bird by Allah's*

Leave; and I heal him who was born blind, and the leper, and I bring the dead to life by Allah's Leave. And I inform you of what you eat, and what you store in your houses. Surely, therein is a sign for you, if you believe. And I have come confirming that which was before me of the Taurat (Torah), and to make lawful to you part of what was forbidden to you, and I have come to you with a proof from your Lord. So fear Allah and obey me. Truly! Allah is my Lord and your Lord, so worship Him (Alone). This is the Straight Path." Then when Isa (Jesus) came to know of their disbelief, he said: "Who will be my helpers in Allah's Cause?" Al-Hawariyyun (the disciples) said: "We are the helpers of Allah; we believe in Allah, and bear witness that we are Muslims (i.e. we submit to Allah). Our Lord! We believe in what you have sent down, and we follow the Messenger [(Isa (Jesus)]; so write us down among those who bear witness (to the truth i.e. La ilaha illallah - none has the right to be worshipped but Allah)" (Quran 3:49-53).

Disciples are also mentioned in Surah Al-Maida where they demand a table full of food:

And when I (Allah) revealed to Al-Hawariyyun (the disciples) [of 'Îsa (Jesus)] to believe in Me and My Messenger, they said: "We believe. And bear witness that we are Muslims." (Remember) when Al-Hawariyyun (the disciples) said: "O 'Îsa (Jesus), son of Maryam (Mary)! Can your Lord send down to us a table spread (with food) from heaven?" Isa (Jesus) said: "Fear Allah, if you are indeed believers." They said: "We wish to eat thereof and to satisfy our hearts (to be stronger in Faith), and to know that you have indeed told us the truth and that we ourselves be its witnesses."

Isa (Jesus), son of Maryam (Mary), said: "O Allah, our Lord! Send us from the heaven a table spread (with food) that there may be for us—for the first and the last of us—a festival and a sign from You; and provide us sustenance, for You are the Best of sustainers." Allah said: "I am going to send it down unto you, but if any of you after that disbelieves, then I will punish him with a torment such as I have not inflicted on anyone among (all) the 'Alamin (mankind and jinn)" (Quran 5:111-115).

And then Allah mentions them in Surah Saff in the Quran:

O you who believe! Be you helpers (in the Cause) of Allah as said 'Isa (Jesus), son of Maryam (Mary), to the Hawariyyun (the disciples): "Who are my helpers (in the Cause) of Allah?" The Hawariyyun (the disciples) said: "We are Allah's helpers" (i.e. we will strive in His Cause!). Then a group of the Children of Israel believed and a group disbelieved. So we gave power to those who believed against their enemies, and they became the victorious (uppermost)" (Quran 61:14).

As mentioned in the Quran, Jesus' true disciples were pious and truthful people. However, the writings of the true disciples of Jesus have either been partially changed or they have been completely replaced by the writings of other people. Christians claim that the New Testament was written by these disciples with the inspiration of the Holy Ghost. According to Christians, people who wrote the New Testament are:

1. Matthew

2. Mark
3. Luke
4. John
5. Paul
6. Peter
7. James
8. Judah

Upon hearing these names as disciples of Jesus, one assumes that all these men had close contact with Jesus and that they spent some time with him. While exploring the background of these disciples, a biblical but Muslim scholar Munquith ibn Mahmoun As-Saqqaar says:

> *The New Testament is a collection of four Gospels, the book of Acts, the twenty one Epistles, and Apocalypse (Revelation), which are the content of the Christians' sacred book. These books are attributed to eight writers who lived in the first and the second generations of Christianity: Matthew, Mark, Luke and John, the writers of Gospels, Paul, the writer of fourteen epistles, and Peter, James and Judah, to whom some epistles are attributed.*
>
> *Matthew, John, Peter, James and Judah were Jesus' (Pbuh) disciples. Mark was Peter's student, and Paul became Christian after Jesus' time, and they never met him in person. Luke, who was Paul's student, became Christian by Paul, who as we mentioned did not meet Jesus (As-Saqqaar, Munqith ibn Mahmud, p. 5).*

7 Death of Jesus

Beliefs surrounding the events of the death of Jesus differ between Christians and Jews. The Quran clearly states that Jesus never died and instead was ascended to heaven by Allah.

In his book *"Qasas-ul-Anbiya (Stories of Prophets)"* Ibn Kathir has narrated the story of Jesus in detail. According to him a group of Jews conspired against Jesus because he was a potential threat to their materialistic interest and Jesus' message was driving people away from their "establishment". Jesus was also questioning the way Jews were interpreting the Jewish sacred revelations and provided many clarifications to that effect. Ibn Kathir writes:

> *"Like an opposing force, the message of Jesus came to denounce the practices of the Pharisees and to reinforce the Law of Moses. In the face of a materialistic age of luxury and worship of gold, Jesus called his people to a nobler life by word and deed. This exemplary life was the only way out of the wretchedness and diseases of his age. Jesus' call, from the beginning, was marked by its complete uprightness and piety. It appealed to the soul, the inner being, and not be a closed system of rules laid down by society.*
>
> *Jesus continued inviting the people to Almighty Allah. His call was based on the principle that there is no mediation between the Creator and His creatures. However, Jesus was in conflict with (some of) the Jews' superficial interpretation of the Torah. He said that he did not come to*

abrogate the Torah, but to complete it by going to the spirit of its substance to arrive at its essence.

He made the Jews understand that the Ten Commandments have more value than they imagined. For instance, the fifth commandment does not only prohibit physical killing, but all forms of killing; physical, psychological, or spiritual. And the sixth commandment does not prohibit adultery only in the sense of unlawful physical contact between a man and a woman, but also prohibits all forms of unlawful relations or acts that might lead to adultery. The eye commits adultery when it looks at anything with passion.

Jesus was, therefore, in confrontation with the materialistic people. He told them to desist from hypocrisy, show, and false praise. There was no need to hoard wealth in this life. They should not preoccupy themselves with the goods of this passing world; rather they must preoccupy themselves with the affairs of the coming world because it would be everlasting.

Jesus told them that caring for this world is a sin, not fit for pious worshippers. The disbelievers care for it because they do not know a better way. As for the believers, they know that their sustenance is with Allah, so they trust in Him and scorn this world.

Jesus continued to invite people to worship the Only Lord, just as he invited them to purify the heart and soul.

His teaching annoyed the priests, for every word of Jesus was a threat to them and their position, exposing their misdeeds (Kathir I. , Stories of Prophets, p. 186).

It was due to this reason that some Jews tried to conspire against Jesus. They decided to embarrass him and to humiliate him. So they came up with a plan and brought an adulterous woman in front of him and asked him whether she should be stoned to death or not. They knew that doing this would leave Jesus with two choices. On the one side he had mercy and clemency he preached while, on the other side, he had to follow the Mosaic Law which stated that adulteress should be stoned to death. Ibn Kathir has written about this plan in detail:

> *However, the priests started to plot against Jesus. They wanted to embarrass him and to prove that he had come to destroy the Mosaic Law. The Mosaic Law provides that an adulteress be stoned to death. They brought him a Jewish adulteress and asked Jesus: "Does not the law stipulate the stoning of the adulteress?" Jesus answered: "Yes." They said: "This woman is an adulteress." Jesus looked at the woman and then at the priests. He knew that they were more sinful than she. They agreed that she should be killed according to Mosaic Law, and they understood that if he was going to apply Mosaic Law, he would be destroying his own rules of forgiveness and mercy.*

> *Jesus understood their plan. He smiled and assented: "Whoever among you is sinless can stone her." His voice rose in the middle of the Temple, making a new law on adultery, for the sinless to judge sin. There was none eligible; no mortal can judge sin, only Allah the Most Merciful.*

As Jesus left the temple, the woman followed him. She took out a bottle of perfume from her garments, knelt before his feet and washed them with perfume and tears, and then dried his feet with her hair. Jesus turned to the woman and told her to stand up, adding: "O Lord, forgive her sins." He let the priests understand that those who call people to Almighty Allah are not executioners. His call was based on mercy for the people, the aim of all divine calls (Kathir I. , Stories of Prophets, p. 187).

And when this plan failed and Jesus continued to preach, Jews became worried and decided to kill Jesus. Ibn Kathir narrates the story in the following manner:

"The Sanhedrin, the highest judicial and ecclesiastical council of the Jews, began to meet to plot against Jesus. The plan took a new turn. When the Jews failed to stop Jesus' call, they decided to kill him. The chief priests held secret meetings to agree on the best way of getting rid of Jesus. While they were in such a meeting, one of the twelve apostles of Jesus, Judas Iscariot, went to them and asked: "What will you give me if I deliver him to you?" Judas bargained with them until they agreed to give him thirty pieces of silver known as shekels. The plot was laid for the capture and murder of Jesus.

It was said that the high priest of the Jews tore his garment at the meeting, claiming that Jesus had denied Judaism. The tearing of clothes at that time was a sign of disgust.

The priests had no authority to pass the death sentence at that time, so they convinced the Roman governor that Jesus was plotting against the security of the Roman Empire and urged him to take immediate action against him. The governor ordered that Jesus be arrested." (Kathir I. , Stories of Prophets, p. 187).

After these orders were given, the Roman army started searching for Jesus. According to the Christian version they found him and crucified him. However, the Quran states the story differently. According to the Quran:

And because of their saying (in boast), "We killed Messiah Isa (Jesus), son of Maryam (Mary), the Messenger of Allah," - but they killed him not, nor crucified him, but it appeared so to them [the resemblance of Isa (Jesus) was put over another man (and they killed that man)], and those who differ therein are full of doubts. They have no (certain) knowledge, they follow nothing but conjecture. For surely; they killed him not [i.e. Isa (Jesus), son of Maryam. But Allah raised him [Isa (Jesus)] up (with his body and soul) unto Himself (and he is in the heavens). And Allah is Ever All-Powerful, All-Wise (Quran 4:156-158).

In his tafseer Ibn Kathir has elaborated on this in the following words:

(The Jews) "envied him because of his prophethood and obvious miracles; curing the blind and leprous and bringing the dead back to life, by Allah's leave. He also used to make the

shape of a bird from clay and blow in it, and it became a bird by Allah's leave and flew. `Isa performed other miracles that Allah honored him with, yet the Jews defied and belied him and tried their best to harm him. Allah's Prophet `Isa could not live in any one city for long and he had to travel often with his mother, peace be upon them. Even so, the Jews were not satisfied, and they went to the king of Damascus at that time, a Greek polytheist who worshipped the stars. They told him that there was a man in Bayt Al-Maqdis misguiding and dividing the people in Jerusalem and stirring unrest among the king's subjects. The king became angry and wrote to his deputy in Jerusalem to arrest the rebel leader, stop him from causing unrest, crucify him and make him wear a crown of thorns. When the king's deputy in Jerusalem received these orders, he went with some Jews to the house that `Isa was residing in, and he was then with twelve, thirteen or seventeen of his companions. That day was a Friday, in the evening. They surrounded `Isa in the house, and when he felt that they would soon enter the house or that he would sooner or later have to leave it, he said to his companions, "Who volunteers to be made to look like me, for which he will be my companion in Paradise." A young man volunteered, but `Isa thought that he was too young. He asked the question a second and third time, each time the young man volunteering, prompting `Isa to say, "Well then, you will be that man." Allah made the young man look exactly like `Isa, while a hole opened in the roof of the house, and `Isa was made to sleep and ascended to heaven while asleep. Allah said, "O `Isa! I will take you and raise you to myself." When `Isa ascended, those who were in the house came out. When those surrounding the house saw the man who looked like `Isa, they thought that he was

'Isa. So they took him at night, crucified him and placed a crown of thorns on his head. The Jews then boasted that they killed 'Isa and some Christians accepted their false claim, due to their ignorance and lack of reason. As for those who were in the house with 'Isa, they witnessed his ascension to heaven, while the rest thought that the Jews killed 'Isa by crucifixion. They even said that Maryam sat under the corpse of the crucified man and cried, and they say that the dead man spoke to her. All this was a test from Allah for His servants out of His wisdom. Allah explained this matter in the Glorious Quran which He sent to His honorable Messenger, whom He supported with miracles and clear, unequivocal evidence. Allah is the Most Truthful, and He is the Lord of the worlds Who knows the secrets, what the hearts conceal, the hidden matters in heaven and earth, what has occurred, what will occur, and what would occur if it was decreed (Kathir I. , Tafsir Ibn Kathir).

At another place in his Tafseer, Ibn Kathir narrates the same story and links it to Muslims:

Ibn Abi Hatim recorded that Ibn 'Abbas said, "Just before Allah raised 'Isa to the heavens, 'Isa went to his companions, who were twelve inside the house. When he arrived, his hair was dripping water and he said, 'There are those among you who will disbelieve in me twelve times after he had believed in me.' He then asked, 'Who volunteers that his image appear as mine, and be killed in my place. He will be with me (in Paradise).' One of the youngest ones among them *volunteered and `Isa asked him to sit down. `Isa again asked for a volunteer, and the young man kept volunteering and `Isa asking him to sit down. Then the young man volunteered again and `Isa said, 'You will be that man,' and the resemblance of `Isa was cast over that man while `Isa ascended to heaven from a hole in the house. When the Jews came looking for `Isa, they found that young man and crucified him. Some of `Isa's followers disbelieved in him twelve times after they had believed in him. They then divided into three groups. One group, Al-Ya`qubiyyah (Jacobites), said, 'Allah remained with us as long as He willed and then ascended to heaven.' Another group, An-Nasturiyyah (Nestorians), said, 'The son of Allah was with us as long as he willed and Allah took him to heaven.' Another group, Muslims, said, 'The servant and Messenger of Allah remained with us as long as Allah willed, and Allah then took him to Him.' The two disbelieving groups cooperated against the Muslim group and they killed them. Ever since that happened, Islam was then veiled until Allah sent Muhammad.'" This statement has an authentic chain of narration leading to Ibn `Abbas, and An-Nasa'i narrated it through Abu Kurayb who reported it from Abu Mu`awiyah (Kathir I. , Tafsir Ibn Kathir, p. 771).*

In his article "Before Nicea" Abdul-Haq ibn Kofi ibn Kwesi ibn al-Ashanti has provided another reference to the same event. According to him:

Some of the first groups that followed the way of Jesus and also several other historical sources other than the Quran confirm that Jesus did not die on the cross. John Toland in his work 'The Nazarenes' mentions that Plotinus who lived in the 4th century stated that he had read a book called

'The Journeys of the Apostles', which related traditions of Peter, John, Andrew, Thomas and Paul. Among other things, the book stated that Jesus was not crucified, but rather another in his place, and therefore, Jesus and the apostles had laughed at those who believed Jesus had died on the cross. Similar was the belief of Basileides and his followers/students who were known as the Basildians.

8   The second coming of Jesus

According to the Quran, Jesus did not die on the cross. He was raised to heavens by Allah and he will return before the Day of Judgment. After his return he will follow Prophet Muhammad's (pbuh) teachings and he will negate the Christian claim that he was crucified. According to Islamic belief, therefore, his return to the world will prove that the Islamic perspective on Jesus was correct and that Islam is the true religion of Allah.

In his book *"Before Nicea,"* Abdul haq ibn Kofi states the following:

> **Eesa (Jesus) (peace be upon him) did not die, rather Allah raised him up to Himself, and he will descend before the Day of Resurrection and will follow Muhammad (peace and blessings of Allah be upon him). He will prove the Jews to be wrong in their claim to have killed 'Eesa and crucified him. And he will prove the Christians to be wrong who exaggerated about him and said that he was God, or the son of God, or the third of three** *(Ashanti, 2005).*

The Prophet (peace and blessings of Allah be upon him) said:

> **The Hour will not be established until the son of Mary (i.e. Jesus) descends amongst you as a just ruler; he will break the cross, kill the pigs, and abolish the Jizya tax. Money will be in abundance so that nobody will accept it (as charitable gifts)** *(Bukhari, p. #Hadith 656 #book 43).*

In another Hadith, Prophet Muhammad (Pbuh) said:

> *I am the closest of people to 'Issa ibn Maryam because there was no Prophet between him and me. . .*

Then he mentioned his descent at the end of time:

> *And he will remain for as long as Allah wills he should remain, then he will die and the Muslims will offer the funeral prayer for him and bury him (al-Albaani, p. #hadith 2182).*

In Quran, Allah stated:

> *And there is none of the people of the Scripture (Jews and Christians) but must believe in him [Isa (Jesus), son of Maryam (Mary), as only a Messenger of Allah and a human being] before him [Isa (Jesus)) or a Jew's or a Christian's] death (at the time of the appearance of the angel of death). And on the Day of Resurrection, he [Isa (Jesus)] will be a witness against them (Quran 4:159).*

This means that Jesus will come back before the Day of Judgment. According to many interpreters of the Quran, the statement, "there is not one of the people of book but will assuredly believe in him before his death, and on Resurrection Day he will be a witness against them", means that once Jesus comes back, all Christians and Jews will believe in him before he dies.

Dr Maneh Hammed states in his essay, "The Truth about Jesus":

The Muslims do believe in and are awaiting for the Second Coming of Jesus. He'll come back not as God to judge the non-Christians, but as Jesus, God's servant. His coming is to correct the misconception which people have developed about his personality and his mission. Al-Bukhaari (3435) and Muslim (28) narrated from 'Ubaadah (may Allah be pleased with him) that the Prophet (peace and blessings of Allah be upon him) said: "Whoever bears witness that there is no god but Allah alone, with no partner or associate, and that Muhammad is His slave and Messenger, and that 'Eesa is His slave and Messenger, a word which Allah bestowed upon Maryam and a spirit created by Him, and that Paradise is real, and Hell is real, Allah will admit him through whichever of the eight gates of Paradise he wishes" (Johani).

9 CONCLUSION

Jesus (Isa) is an important figure both for Christians and Muslims. The Quran includes many references to Jesus and Allah's special blessings that he bestowed upon him and his family, especially Maryam (Mary). Appendix A provides verses of the Quran where Jesus (Isa) and Maryam is mentioned. The appendix also includes the full Chapter of Maryam from the Quran.

10 Appendix A – Quranic verses and Chapter on Mary (Maryam) and Jesus (Isa)

The following are some verses that mention Jesus and Mary in the Quran.

10.1 Chapter of Baqara Quran Verses (Chapter 2)

"And We gave 'Eesa (Jesus), the son of Maryam (Mary), clear signs and supported him with Rooh-ul-Qudus [Jibreel (Gabriel)]

---- [Al-Baqarah 2:87)]

"And they (Jews, Christians and pagans) say: Allah has begotten a son (Children or offspring). Glory be to Him (Exalted be He above all that they associate with Him). Nay, to Him belongs all that is in the heavens and on earth, and all surrender with obedience (in worship) to Him", "The Originator of the heavens and the earth. When He decrees a matter, He only says to it: "Be!" and it is".

---- [Chapter 2: verses 116-17]

"Say (O Muslims), "We believe in Allah and that which has been sent down to us and that which has been sent down to Ibrahim (Abraham), Ismail (Ishmael), Ishaque (Isaac), Yaqoob (Jacob), and to Al-Asbat (the twelve sons of Yaqoob (Jacob)), and that which has been given to Moosa (Moses) and Iesa (Jesus), and that which has been given to the Prophets from their Lord. We make no distinction between any of them, and to Him we have

66

submitted (in Islam)."

---- [Al-Baqara, 2: 136]

"And your Ilah (God) is One Ilah (God - Allah), La ilaha illa Huwa (there is none who has the right to be worshipped but He), the Most Beneficent, the Most Merciful.

---- [Al-Baqara, 2:163]

"And of mankind are some who take (for worship) others besides Allah as rivals (to Allah). They love them as they love Allah. But those who believe, love Allah more (than anything else). If only, those who do wrong could see, when they will see the torment, that all power belongs to Allah and that Allah is Severe in punishment."

---- [Al-Baqara, 2: 165). ."

"Those Messengers! We preferred some of them to others; to some of them Allâh spoke (directly); others He raised to degrees (of honour); and to 'Eesa (Jesus), the son of Maryam (Mary), We gave clear proofs and evidences, and supported him with Rooh ul Qudus [Jibreel (Gabriel)]"

---- (Al-Baqarah 2:253)]

10.2 Chapter Aal-Imraan Quran Verses (Chapter 3)

"And (remember) when the angels said: 'O Maryam (Mary)! Verily, Allaah has chosen you, purified you (from polytheism and disbelief), and chosen you above the women of the 'Aalameen (mankind and jinn) (of her lifetime).'

O Maryam! 'Submit yourself with obedience to your Lord (Allaah, by worshipping none but Him Alone) and prostrate yourself, and bow down along with Ar-Raaki'oon (those who bow down)'"

---- [Aal 'Imraan 3:42-43]

"(Remember) when the angels said: 'O Maryam (Mary)! Verily, Allaah gives you the glad tidings of a Word ["Be!" — and he was! i.e. 'Eesa (Jesus) the son of Maryam (Mary)] from Him, his name will be the Messiah 'Eesa (Jesus), the son of Maryam (Mary), held in honour in this world and in the Hereafter, and will be one of those who are near to Allaah.

He will speak to the people, in the cradle and in manhood, and he will be one of the righteous.'

She said: 'O my Lord! How shall I have a son when no man has touched me.' He said: 'So (it will be) for Allaah creates what He wills. When He has decreed something, He says to it only: "Be!" and it is'"

---- [Aal 'Imraan 3:45-47]

"And He (Allaah) will teach him ['Eesa (Jesus)] the Book

and Al-Hikmah (i.e. the Sunnah, the faultless speech of the Prophets, wisdom), (and) the Tawraat (Torah) and the Injeel (Gospel).

And will make him ['Eesa (Jesus)] a Messenger to the Children of Israel (saying): 'I have come to you with a sign from your Lord, that I design for you out of clay, a figure like that of a bird, and breathe into it, and it becomes a bird by Allaah's Leave; and I heal him who was born blind, and the leper, and I bring the dead to life by Allaah's Leave. And I inform you of what you eat, and what you store in your houses. Surely, therein is a sign for you, if you believe.

---- [Aal 'Imraan 3:48-49]

"Then when 'Eesa (Jesus) came to know of their disbelief, he said: 'Who will be my helpers in Allaah's Cause?' Al-Hawaariyyoon (the disciples) said: 'We are the helpers of Allaah; we believe in Allaah, and bear witness that we are Muslims (i.e. we submit to Allaah).'

Our Lord! We believe in what You have sent down, and we follow the Messenger ['Eesa (Jesus)]; so write us down among those who bear witness (to the truth, i.e. Laa ilaaha illallaah — none has the right to be worshipped but Allaah)"

---- [Aal 'Imraan 3:52-53]

"Verily, the likeness of 'Eesa (Jesus) before Allaah is the likeness of Adam. He created him from dust, then (He) said to him: 'Be!' — and he was".

---- [Aal 'Imraan 3:59]

"Verily! This is the true narrative [about the story of 'Isa (Jesus)], and, Laa ilaaha ill-
Allah (none has the right to be worshipped but Allah, the One and the Only True
God, Who has neither a wife nor a son). And indeed, Allah is the All-Mighty, the
All-Wise.

---- [Aal 'Imraan 3:62]

10.3 Chapter of Al-Nisaa Quran Verses (Chapter 4)

"And because of their saying (in boast), 'We killed Messiah 'Eesa (Jesus), son of Maryam (Mary), the Messenger of Allaah,' — but they killed him not, nor crucified him, but it appeared so to them the resemblance of 'Eesa (Jesus) was put over another man (and they killed that man)], and those who differ therein are full of doubts. They have no (certain) knowledge, they follow nothing but conjecture. For surely; they killed him not [i.e. 'Eesa (Jesus), son of Maryam (Mary)]:

But Allaah raised him ['Eesa (Jesus)] up (with his body and soul) unto Himself (and he is in the heavens). And Allaah is Ever All Powerful, All Wise"

---- [al-Nisaa' 4:157-158]

"And there is none of the people of the Scripture (Jews and Christians) but must believe in him ['Eesa (Jesus), son of Maryam (Mary), as only a Messenger of Allaah

and a human being] before his ['Eesa (Jesus) or a Jew's or a Christian's] death (at the time of the appearance of the angel of death). And on the Day of Resurrection, he ['Eesa (Jesus)] will be a witness against them"

---- [al-Nisaa' 4:159]

"O people of the Scripture (Jews and Christians)! Do not exceed the limits in your religion, nor say of Allah aught but the truth. The Messiah Iesa (Jesus), son of Maryam (Mary), was (no more than) a Messenger of Allah and His Word, ("Be!" - and he was) which He bestowed on Maryam (Mary) and a spirit (Rooh) created by Him; so believe in Allah and His Messengers. Say not: "Three (trinity)!" Cease! (it is) better for you. For Allah is (the only) One Ilah (God), Glory be to Him (Far Exalted is He) above having a son. To Him belongs all that is in the heavens and all that is in the earth. And Allah is AllSufficient as a Disposer of affairs."

---- [an-Nisaa: 4:171]

10.4 Chapter Al-Maaidah Quran Verses (Chapter 5)

"and We gave him the Injeel (Gospel), in which was guidance and light and confirmation of the Tawraat (Torah) that had come before it, a guidance and an admonition for Al-Muttaqoon (the pious)"

---- [al-Maa'idah 5:46]

"Surely, they have disbelieved who say: "Allah is the

Messiah (Iesa (Jesus)), son of Maryam (Mary)." But the
Messiah (Iesa (Jesus)) said: "O Children of Israel!
Worship Allah, my Lord and your Lord." Verily,
whosoever sets up partners in worship with Allah, then
Allah has forbidden Paradise for him, and the Fire will
be his abode. And for the Zalimoon (polytheists and
wrongdoers) there are no helpers."

---- [al-Maa'idah 5:72]

"Surely, disbelievers are those who said: 'Allaah is the
third of the three (in a Trinity)." But there is no Ilaah
(god) (none who has the right to be worshipped) but One
Ilaah (God —Allaah). And if they cease not from what
they say, verily, a painful torment will befall on the
disbelievers among them"

---- [al-Maa'idah 5:73]

"The Messiah ['Eesa (Jesus)], son of Maryam (Mary),
was no more than a Messenger; many were the
Messengers that passed away before him. His mother
[Maryam (Mary)] was a Siddeeqah [i.e. she believed in
the Words of Allaah and His Books]. They both used to
eat food (as any other human being, while Allaah does
not eat). Look how We make the Ayaat (proofs,
evidences, verses, lessons, signs, revelations, etc.)
clear to them; yet look how they are deluded away (from
the truth)"

---- [al-Maa'idah 5:75]

"Verily, you will find the strongest among men in enmity to the believers (Muslims) the Jews and those who are Al-Mushrikoon, and you will find the nearest in love to the believers (Muslims) those who say: 'We are Christians.' That is because amongst them are priests and monks, and they are not proud"

---- [al-Maa'idah 5:82]

"O 'Eesa (Jesus), son of Maryam (Mary)! Remember My Favour to you and to your mother when I supported you with Rooh ul Qudus [Jibreel (Gabriel)]..."

---- (Al-Maa'idah 5:110)

"And (remember) when Allaah will say (on the Day of Resurrection): 'O 'Eesa (Jesus), son of Maryam (Mary)! Did you say unto men: "Worship me and my mother as two gods besides Allaah?"' He will say: 'Glory be to You! It was not for me to say what I had no right (to say). Had I said such a thing, You would surely have known it. You know what is in my inner-self though I do not know what is in Yours; truly, You, only You, are the All-Knower of all that is hidden (and unseen).

Never did I say to them aught except what You (Allaah) did command me to say: "Worship Allaah, my Lord and your Lord."' And I was a witness over them while I dwelt amongst them, but when You took me up, You were the Watcher over them; and You are a Witness to all things. (This is a great admonition and warning to the Christians of the whole world).

If You punish them, they are Your slaves, and if You

forgive them, verily, You, only You, are the All Mighty, the All Wise"'

---- [al-Maa'idah, 5:116-118]

10.5 Chapter Al-Aaraf Quran Verses (Chapter 7)

And (remember) when your Lord brought forth from the Children of Adam, from their loins, their seed (or from Adams loin his offspring) and made them testify as to themselves (saying): "Am I not your Lord?" They said: "Yes! We testify," lest you should say on the Day of Resurrection: "Verily, we have been unaware of this."

---- [al-A'raaf, (7):172)]

10.6 Chapter Al-Nahl Quran Verses (Chapter 16)

"Say (O Muhammad) Rooh ul Qudus [Jibreel (Gabriel)] has brought it (the Qur'aan) down from your Lord with truth, that it may make firm and strengthen (the Faith of) those who believe, and as a guidance and glad tidings to those who have submitted (to Allaah as Muslims)"

---- [(Al-Nahl 16:102)]

10.7 Chapter Ash-Shuara Quran Verses (Chapter 26)

"..Which the trustworthy Rooh [Jibreel (Gabriel)] has brought down

---- (Ash-Shu'ara' 26:193)

10.8 Chapter Ash-Shura Quran Verses (Chapter 42)

"He (Allah) has ordained for you the same religion (Islam) which He ordained for Nooh (Noah), and that which We have inspired in you (O Muhammad SAW), and that which We ordained for Ibraheem (Abraham), Moosa (Moses) and Iesa (Jesus) saying you should establish religion (i.e. to do what it orders you to do practically), and make no divisions in it (religion) (i.e. various sects in religion). Intolerable for the Mushrikoon , is that to which you (O Muhammad SAW) call them. Allah chooses for Himself whom He wills, and guides unto Himself who turns to Him in repentance and in obedience."

---- [Ash-Shura, 42: 13]

10.9 Chapter As-Saff Quran Verses (Chapter 61)

"And (remember) when 'Eesa (Jesus), son of Maryam (Mary), said: 'O Children of Israel! I am the Messenger of Allaah unto you, confirming the Tawraat [(Torah) which came] before me, and giving glad tidings of a Messenger to come after me, whose name shall be Ahmad.' But when he (Ahmad, i.e. Muhammad) came to them with clear proofs, they said: 'This is plain magic'"

---- [as-Saff 61:6]

10.10 Chapter of Maryam (Mary) – Complete (Chapter 19)

1. Kaf- Ha-Ya-'Ain-Sad. [These letters are one of the miracles of the Quran, and none but Allah (Alone) knows their meanings].

2. (This is) a mention of the mercy of your Lord to His slave Zakariya (Zachariah).

3. When he called out his Lord (Allah) a call in secret,

4. Saying: "My Lord! Indeed my bones have grown feeble, and grey hair has spread on my head, And I have never been unblest in my invocation to You, O my Lord!

5. "And Verily! I fear my relatives after me, since my wife is barren. So give me from Yourself an heir,

6. "Who shall inherit me, and inherit (also) the posterity of Ya'qub (Jacob) (inheritance of the religious knowledge and Prophethood, not the wealth, etc.). And make him, my Lord, one with whom You are Well-pleased!".

7. (Allah said) "O Zakariya (Zachariah)! Verily, We give you the glad tidings of a son, His name will be Yahya (John). We have given that name to none before (him)."

8. He said: "My Lord! How can I have a son, when my wife is barren, and I have reached the extreme old age."

9. He said: "So (it will be). Your Lord says; It is easy for Me. Certainly I have created you before, when you had been nothing!"

10. [Zakariya (Zachariah)] said: "My Lord! Appoint for me a sign." He said: "Your sign is that you shall not speak unto mankind for three nights, though having no bodily defect."

11. Then he came out to his people from Al-Mihrab (a praying place or a private room, etc.), he told them by signs to glorify Allah's Praises in the morning and in the afternoon.

12. (It was said to his son): "O Yahya (John)! Hold fast the Scripture [the Taurat (Torah)]." And We gave him wisdom while yet a child.

13. And (made him) sympathetic to men as a mercy (or a grant) from Us, and pure from sins [i.e. Yahya (John)] and he was righteous,

14. And dutiful towards his parents, and he was neither an arrogant nor disobedient (to Allah or to his parents).

15. And Salamun (peace) be on him the day he was born, the day he dies, and the day he will be raised up to life (again)!

16. And mention in the Book (the Quran, O Muhammad , the story of) Maryam (Mary), when she withdrew in seclusion from her family to a place facing east.

17. She placed a screen (to screen herself) from them; then We sent to her Our Ruh [angel Jibrael (Gabriel)], and he appeared before her in the form of a man in all respects.

18. She said: "Verily! I seek refuge with the Most Beneficent (Allah) from you, if you do fear Allah."

19. (The angel) said: "I am only a Messenger from your

Lord, (to announce) to you the gift of a righteous son."

20. She said: "How can I have a son, when no man has touched me, nor am I unchaste?"

21. He said: "So (it will be), your Lord said: 'That is easy for Me (Allah): And (We wish) to appoint him as a sign to mankind and a mercy from Us (Allah), and it is a matter (already) decreed, (by Allah).' "

22. So she conceived him, and she withdrew with him to a far place (i.e. Bethlehem valley about 4-6 miles from Jerusalem).

23. And the pains of childbirth drove her to the trunk of a date-palm. She said: "Would that I had died before this, and had been forgotten and out of sight!"

24. Then [the babe 'Iesa (Jesus) or Jibrael (Gabriel)] cried unto her from below her, saying: "Grieve not! Your Lord has provided a water stream under you;

25. "And shake the trunk of date-palm towards you, it will let fall fresh ripe-dates upon you."

26. "So eat and drink and be glad, and if you see any human being, say: 'Verily! I have vowed a fast unto the Most Beneficent (Allah) so I shall not speak to any human being this day.'"

27. Then she brought him (the baby) to her people, carrying him. They said: "O Mary! Indeed you have brought a thing Fariya (an unheard mighty thing).

28. "O sister (i.e. the like) of Harun (Aaron) [not the brother of Musa (Moses), but he was another pious man at the time of Maryam (Mary)]! Your father was not a man who used to commit adultery, nor your mother was an unchaste woman."

29. Then she pointed to him. They said: "How can we talk to one who is a child in the cradle?"

30. "He ['Iesa (Jesus)] said: Verily! I am a slave of Allah, He has given me the Scripture and made me a Prophet;"

31. "And He has made me blessed wheresoever I be, and has enjoined on me Salat (prayer), and Zakat, as long as I live."

32. "And dutiful to my mother, and made me not arrogant, unblest.

33. "And Salam (peace) be upon me the day I was born, and the day I die, and the day I shall be raised alive!"

34. Such is 'Iesa (Jesus), son of Maryam (Mary). (it is) a statement of truth, about which they doubt (or dispute).

35. It befits not (the Majesty of) Allah that He should beget a son [this refers to the slander of Christians against Allah, by saying that 'Iesa (Jesus) is the son of Allah]. Glorified (and Exalted be He above all that they associate with Him). When He decrees a thing, He only says to it, "Be!" and it is.

36. ['Iesa (Jesus) said]: "And verily Allah is my Lord and your Lord. So worship Him (Alone). That is the Straight Path. (Allah's Religion of Islamic Monotheism which He did ordain for all of His Prophets)." [Tafsir At-Tabari]

37. Then the sects differed [i.e. the Christians about 'Iesa (Jesus)], so woe unto the disbelievers [those who gave false witness by saying that 'Iesa (Jesus) is the son of Allah] from the meeting of a great Day (i.e. the Day of Resurrection, when they will be thrown in the blazing

Fire).

38. How clearly will they (polytheists and disbelievers in the Oneness of Allah) see and hear, the Day when they will appear before Us! But the Zalimun (polytheists and wrong-doers) today are in plain error.

39. And warn them (O Muhammad) of the Day of grief and regrets, when the case has been decided, while (now) they are in a state of carelessness, and they believe not.

40. Verily! We will inherit the earth and whatsoever is thereon. And to Us they all shall be returned,

41. And mention in the Book (the Quran) Ibrahim (Abraham). Verily! He was a man of truth, a Prophet.

42. When he said to his father: "O my father! Why do you worship that which hears not, sees not and cannot avail you in anything?

43. "O my father! Verily! There has come to me of knowledge that which came not unto you. So follow me. I will guide you to a Straight Path.

44. "O my father! Worship not Shaitan (Satan). Verily! Shaitan (Satan) has been a rebel against the Most Beneficent (Allah).

45. "O my father! Verily! I fear lest a torment from the Most Beneficent (Allah) overtake you, so that you become a companion of Shaitan (Satan) (in the Hell-fire)." [Tafsir Al-Qurtubi]

46. He (the father) said: "Do you reject my gods, O Ibrahim (Abraham)? If you stop not (this), I will indeed stone you. So get away from me safely before I punish you."

47. Ibrahim (Abraham) said: "Peace be on you! I will ask Forgiveness of my Lord for you. Verily! He is unto me, Ever Most Gracious.

48. "And I shall turn away from you and from those whom you invoke besides Allah. And I shall call on my Lord; and I hope that I shall not be unblest in my invocation to my Lord."

49. So when he had turned away from them and from those whom they worshipped besides Allah, We gave him Ishaque (Isaac) and Ya'qub (Jacob), and each one of them We made a Prophet.

50. And We gave them of Our Mercy (a good provision in plenty), and We granted them honour on the tongues (of all the nations, i.e everybody remembers them with a good praise).

51. And mention in the Book (this Quran) Musa (Moses). Verily! He was chosen and he was a Messenger (and) a Prophet.

52. And We called him from the right side of the Mount, and made him draw near to Us for a talk with him [Musa (Moses)].

53. And We bestowed on him his brother Harun (Aaron), (also) a Prophet, out of Our Mercy.

54. And mention in the Book (the Quran) Isma'il (Ishmael). Verily! He was true to what he promised, and he was a Messenger, (and) a Prophet.

55. And he used to enjoin on his family and his people As-Salat (the prayers) and the Zakat, and his Lord was pleased with him.

56. And mention in the Book (the Quran) Idris (Enoch).Verily! He was a man of truth, (and) a Prophet.

57. And We raised him to a high station.

58. Those were they unto whom Allah bestowed His Grace from among the Prophets, of the offspring of Adam, and of those whom We carried (in the ship) with Nuh (Noah), and of the offspring of Ibrahim (Abraham) and Israel and from among those whom We guided and chose. When the Verses of the Most Beneficent (Allah) were recited unto them, they fell down prostrating and weeping.

59. Then, there has succeeded them a posterity who have given up As-Salat (the prayers) [i.e. made their Salat (prayers) to be lost, either by not offering them or by not offering them perfectly or by not offering them in their proper fixed times, etc.] and have followed lusts. So they will be thrown in Hell.

60. Except those who repent and believe (in the Oneness of Allah and His Messenger Muhammad), and work righteousness. Such will enter Paradise and they will not be wronged in aught.

61. (They will enter) 'Adn (Eden) Paradise (everlasting Gardens), which the Most Beneficent (Allah) has promised to His slaves in the unseen: Verily! His Promise must come to pass.

62. They shall not hear therein (in Paradise) any Laghw (dirty, false, evil vain talk), but only Salam (salutations of peace). And they will have therein their sustenance, morning and afternoon. [See (V.40:55)].

63. *Such is the Paradise which We shall give as an inheritance to those of Our slaves who have been Al-Muttaqun (pious and righteous persons - See V.2:2).*

64. *And we (angels) descend not except by the Command of your Lord (O Muhammad). To Him belongs what is before us and what is behind us, and what is between those two, and your Lord is never forgetful,*

65. *Lord of the heavens and the earth, and all that is between them, so worship Him (Alone) and be constant and patient in His worship. Do you know of any who is similar to Him? (of course none is similar or coequal or comparable to Him, and He has none as partner with Him). [There is nothing like unto Him and He is the All-Hearer, the All-Seer].*

66. *And man (the disbeliever) says: "When I am dead, shall I then be raised up alive?"*

67. *Does not man remember that We created him before, while he was nothing?*

68. *So by your Lord, surely, We shall gather them together, and (also) the Shayatin (devils) (with them), then We shall bring them round Hell on their knees.*

69. *Then indeed We shall drag out from every sect all those who were worst in obstinate rebellion against the Most Beneficent (Allah).*

70. *Then, verily, We know best those who are most worthy of being burnt therein.*

71. *There is not one of you but will pass over it (Hell); this is with your Lord; a Decree which must be accomplished.*

72. *Then We shall save those who use to fear Allah and were dutiful to Him. And We shall leave the Zalimun (polytheists and wrongdoers, etc.) therein (humbled) to their knees (in Hell).*

73. *And when Our Clear Verses are recited to them, those who disbelieve (the rich and strong among the pagans of Quraish who live a life of luxury) say to those who believe (the weak, poor companions of Prophet Muhammad who have a hard life): "Which of the two groups (i.e. believers and disbelievers) is best in (point of) position and as regards station (place of council for consultation)."*

74. *And how many a generation (past nations) have We destroyed before them, who were better in wealth, goods and outward appearance?*

75. *Say (O Muhammad) whoever is in error, the Most Beneficent (Allah) will extend (the rope) to him, until, when they see that which they were promised, either the torment or the Hour, they will come to know who is worst in position, and who is weaker in forces. [This is the answer for the Verse No.19:73]*

76. *And Allah increases in guidance those who walk aright [true believers in the Oneness of Allah who fear Allah much (abstain from all kinds of sins and evil deeds which He has forbidden), and love Allah much (perform all kinds of good deeds which He has ordained)]. And the righteous good deeds that last, are better with your Lord, for reward and better for resort.*

77. *Have you seen him who disbelieved in Our Ayat (this Quran and Muhammad) and (yet) says: "I shall certainly be given wealth and children [if I will be alive (again)],"*

78. *Has he known the unseen or has he taken a*

covenant from the Most Beneficent (Allah)?

79. Nay! We shall record what he says, and We shall increase his torment (in the Hell);

80. And We shall inherit from him (at his death) all that he talks of (i.e. wealth and children which We have bestowed upon him in this world), and he shall come to Us alone.

81. And they have taken (for worship) aliha (gods) besides Allah, that they might give them honour, power and glory (and also protect them from Allah's Punishment etc.).

82. Nay, but they (the so-called gods) will deny their worship of them, and become opponents to them (on the Day of Resurrection).

83. See you not that We have sent the Shayatin (devils) against the disbelievers to push them to do evil.

84. So make no haste against them; We only count out to them a (limited) number (of the days of the life of this world and delay their term so that they may increase in evil and sins).

85. The Day We shall gather the Muttaqun (pious - see V.2:2) unto the Most Beneficent (Allah), like a delegate (presented before a king for honour).

86. And We shall drive the Mujrimun (polytheists, sinners, criminals, disbelievers in the Oneness of Allah, etc.) to Hell, in a thirsty state (like a thirsty herd driven down to water),

87. None shall have the power of intercession, but such a one as has received permission (or promise) from the

Most Beneficent (Allah).

88. And they say: "The Most Beneficent (Allah) has begotten a son (or offspring or children) [as the Jews say: 'Uzair (Ezra) is the son of Allah, and the Christians say that He has begotten a son ['Iesa (Christ)], and the pagan Arabs say that He has begotten daughters (angels, etc.)]."

89. Indeed you have brought forth (said) a terrible evil thing.

90. Whereby the heavens are almost torn, and the earth is split asunder, and the mountains fall in ruins,

91. That they ascribe a son (or offspring or children) to the Most Beneficent (Allah).

92. But it is not suitable for (the Majesty of) the Most Beneficent (Allah) that He should beget a son (or offspring or children).

93. There is none in the heavens and the earth but comes unto the Most Beneficent (Allah) as a slave.

94. Verily, He knows each one of them, and has counted them a full counting.

95. And everyone of them will come to Him alone on the Day of Resurrection (without any helper, or protector or defender).

96. Verily, those who believe [in the Oneness of Allah and in His Messenger (Muhammad)] and work deeds of righteousness, the Most Beneficent (Allah) will bestow love for them (in the hearts of the believers).

97. So We have made this (the Quran) easy in your own

tongue (O Muhammad), only that you may give glad tidings to the Muttaqun (pious and righteous persons - See V.2:2), and warn with it the Ludda (most quarrelsome) people.

98. And how many a generation before them have We destroyed! Can you (O Muhammad) find a single one of them or hear even a whisper of them?

11 REFERENCES

Ajijola, A. *The Hijacking of Chrisitanity.*

Al Hindi, P. F. (n.d.). The biggest debate between Al Hindi and the Priest Fender.

al-Albaani. *Al-Silsala al-Saheehah.*

Ashanti, A. H. (2005). *Before Nicea.* Retrieved 9 2010, 1, from Islamhouse.com:
http://d1.islamhouse.com/data/en/ih_books/single/en_Before_Nicea.pdf

As-Saqqaar, Munqith ibn Mahmud. (n.d.). *Is the New Testament God's word?* (A. A. Omara, Ed., & A. Qassem, Trans.) Retrieved 9 1, 2010, from Islamhouse:
http://d1.islamhouse.com/data/en/ih_books/single/en_IstheNewTestement.pdf

Bukhari, I. (n.d.). *Sahih Bukhari.* Retrieved 9 2010, 1, from searchtruth.com:
http://www.searchtruth.com/searchHadith.php?keyword=pigs&translator=1&search=1&book=&start=0

Debate between Ahmed Deedat and Jimmy Swaggart about the topic "Is the Bible God's? Word". (n.d.). *Video* . U.S.A.

Ehrman, B. (2003). *Lost Christianities.* Oxford University Press.

Grant, F. (n.d.). The Gospels, their origin and their growth.

Holy Quran . (n.d.). (M. Khan, Trans.) Retrieved 9 28, 2010, from www.searchtruth.com.

Johani, D. M. (n.d.). *The Truth about Jesus.* Retrieved 9 2010, 1, from Islamhouse.com:
http://d1.islamhouse.com/data/en/ih_books/signal/en_the_truth_about_messiah.pdf

Kalby, K. A. (2005). *Prophet Muhammad (Pbuh) the Last Messenger in Bible* (8 ed.). (T. H. Bandolin, Trans.)

Kathir, I. In I. Kathir, *Stories of Prophets* (A.-A. Muhammad Mustapha Geme'ah, Trans., p. 178). Riyadh, Saudi Arabaia: Darussalam.

Kathir, I. (n.d.). *Tafseer Ibn-e-Kathir.* Retrieved 9 1, 2010, from Tafsir.com: http://www.tafsir.com/default.asp?sid=3&tid=8277

Kathir, I. (n.d.). *Tafsir Ibn Kathir.* Retrieved 9 1, 2010, from jojobvlgari.wikispaces:
http://jojobvlgari.wikispaces.com/file/view/Tafsir+Ibn+Kathir+all+10+volumes_1.pdf

Lehmann, J. (1972). *The Jesus Report.* London: Souvenir Press.

MD, L. B. (n.d.). *Where is the "Christ" in "Christianity"?* Retrieved 9 1, 2010, from Islamhouse.com:
http://d1.islamhouse.com/data/en/ih_articles/en_WhereistheChristinChristianity.pdf

MD, L. B. (n.d.). *Where is the "Christ" in "Christianity"?* Retrieved 9 1, 2010, from Islamhouse:

http://d1.islamhouse.com/data/en/ih_articles/en_WhereistheChr istinChristianity.pdf

Miskeen, F. M. (n.d.). The Gospel acording to John. *1* .

Muhaimin, R. A. (2003). *Jesus and The Bible.* Retrieved 9 1, 2010, from Islamhouse.com: http://d1.islamhouse.com/data/en/ih_books/single/en_Jesus_the _Bible.pdf

Noor, P. M. *Fake Suspicions about bible.*

Philips, D. B. (1996). *The True Message of Jesus Christ.* Sharjah, U.A.E: Dar Al Fatah Printing, Publishing and distribution Co.

The Biggest debate between Al hindi and the Priest Fender. (n.d.).

wahab, A. A. *Differences between the translations of the Holy Bible.*

Weiss, J. (1909). *Paul and Jesus.* (R. H. Chaytor, Trans.)

Other Books by IqraSense

1. Jerusalem is Ours - The centuries old Christian, Islamic, and Jewish struggle for the "Holy Lands"
2. The Power of Dua (Prayers)
3. 100+ Dua (Prayers) for Success and Happiness
4. Summarized Stories of the Quran

ABOUT THE AUTHOR

IqraSense is an Islamic blog covering topics on Islam and other religions. To discuss this topic in more detail, you are encouraged to join the discussion and provide your comments by visiting the blog.

Made in the USA
San Bernardino, CA
15 August 2015